FOOLS
RUSH
INN

D1568452

FOOLS
RUSH
INN

MORE DETOURS ON THE ROAD
TO CONVENTIONAL WISDOM

by Bill James

FOOLS RUSH INN
More Detours on the Road to Conventional Wisdom
by Bill James

Edited by Gregory F. Augustine Pierce
Cover design by Tom A. Wright
Text design and typesetting by Patricia A. Lynch

Published by ACTA Sports, a division of ACTA Publications,
4848 N. Clark Street, Chicago, IL 60640 (800) 397-2282
www.actasports.com

Library of Congress Number: 2014937594
ISBN: 978-0-87946-497-4
Printed in the United States of America by Total Printing Systems
Year: 25 24 23 22 21 20 19 18 17 16 15 14
Printing: 15 14 13 12 11 10 9 8 7 6 5 4 3 2 First

♻ Black text printed on 30% post-consumer recycled paper

Contents

Introwledgements

by Bill James

———·———

Snatched from the great gulf,
like oysters by bibliomaniac pearl-divers,
there must they first rot, then what was pearl,
in Camille or others, may be seen as such,
and continue as such.

Thomas Carlyle
The French Revolution

———·———

The Core Acknowledgement Cadre for this book is three people—John Dewan, Dave Studenmund and Greg Pierce. This book is...how should we say...an outgrowth or a side effect of Bill James Online. I write probably 40, 50 articles a year for Bill James Online. We charge $3 a month to be a member of BJOL, just to keep the riff-raff out. John Dewan also writes articles for BJOL, and manages the business, and Dave Studenmund manages the site on a day to day basis. Greg Pierce periodically reviews the articles I have published there, selects a few of them which he sees as being worthy of paper and ink, edits them; occasionally we update something if we are re-publishing it after a passage of time. These selected articles become a book. This would be exactly such a book.

When the internet was new there was a perception that what was published on the web was transient and therefore of little significance. I remember that very early, people would say that something was "published" on the web, in quotation marks, as if it had not *really* been published, although in truth this usage of the term "published" is consistent with the very old meaning of the term,

7

which pre-dates the publishing industry. We are beginning to come to terms with the reality that the opposite is true: that that which is published on paper is transient, while that which is published electronically will last forever.

We are in this long transition, where everything which has ever been published on paper and which has managed to survive this long is being saved for the future by creating an electronic image of it. This process will go on for a good many years yet, at least another twenty years, and possibly a hundred. Eventually we will reach the place where the words of the past can be searched at will, as easily as one can swim across an ocean.

That is the problem, that we have made publishing so easy that there is now a totally unmanageable amount of it. Thomas Carlyle was talking about rotting newspapers (I think. When Carlyle really gets rolling, even his most devoted fans can't figure out what in the hell he is talking about.) But he had mentioned newspapers in the previous sentence, and I think what he was talking about was the necessity of letting the old newspapers rot away, so that we can see what is left standing after the bluster and tumult have died away. What do we do when the past no longer rots away, but is left standing to haunt the next millennium like a paper maché ghost?

For two hundred years or more, book publishers have been— apologizing in advance for the grandiosity of the language—book publishers have been the gatekeepers of immortality. It was they who were tasked to figure out what there was among the billions of words written each year that was worth saving for the next generation. It is an awkward irony that, right at the moment when the economic underpinnings are being kicked from beneath the publishers, we find ourselves most in need of people to sort through the piles and figure out what is worth saving. It is unclear who will fill this role in the next generation. The academics would like to do it, collectively, but individually they burn off most of their energy fighting one another for status within their own universe. The people who have the best tools to do it seem to be the most obsessed with making money, and thus tend to immortalize celebrity, rather than wisdom.

Have you ever known anybody who had no internal filter, who would simply say the first thing that came into her head without stopping to think how this might be perceived by others? The world is that woman now, that person who says whatever she has to say, right from the heart, no filters, buddy. When publishing becomes effortless, it gives rise to super-publishing. We sort through what is written after it is published, rather than before. Greg Pierce, then, is not my publisher, because nobody needs a publisher any more, but my super-publisher, my filter-after-the-fact who sorts through my online grunts and groans, my yelps and hollers, looking for a little bit of insight. I appreciate the effort.

The main acknowledgment for the book, in a sense, is the BJOL readers; I don't know most of their names or care to know them, but they are always suggesting things to write about—not directly, in the sense of "You should write about this, Bill James," but by reacting to what was written before, by pointing out what was unsaid before, by seeing different implications of what we have been talking about. They keep the water moving through the stream, and these articles would be like the pools that collect around the edges of the stream. The book was supposed to be called *Pools Rush In*, but there was a typo, and we were never able to get that corrected. That's what Greg told me, anyway.

Thank you all for reading, because I would go crazy in three months if I couldn't write, and without the readers I am afraid I would have to stop writing. Writing is like a drug to me; after 40 years a'writin I still wake up in the middle of the night, anxious to get to the keyboard, and often have to force myself to stay in bed and finish my sleep. Like most writers, I tend to regard everything that happens after the prose leaves my office as mere process at best, interference at worst, but the collapse of the newspaper business and the ever-growing difficulties of the book publishing biz remind us that this is not the case, that nothing is automatic, and editors should not be taken for granted. I appreciate all of your help.

———·———

DIVIDING BASEBALL HISTORY INTO ERAS

by Bill James

I first became aware of the concept of dividing baseball history into eras with the publication of the Neft/Cohen Baseball Encyclopedia. *The Sports Encyclopedia: Baseball (1974)* was a marvelous book in its day. It largely ignored the 19th century—a wise choice—and segmented "modern" baseball history into four eras—the Dead Ball Era (1901-1919), the Lively Ball Era (1920-1945), the Post-War Era (1946-1960), and the Expansion Era (1961-1973). Then it presented, as I recall, a two-page statistical spread about each league each season, with a write-up about the year and some interludes summarizing player's careers. It was a seminal work.

Those era breakdowns worked until about 1980, but after about 1980 they didn't really work anymore. The world decided that 19th century baseball was major league baseball, ignoring all of the obvious indicators to the contrary, and the "post-expansion era" would now stretch to more than half a century if we were still in that. The commissioner's office decided to promote the idea that the arrival of Jackie Robinson was the biggest event in the history of the game. At some point we didn't know where to draw the lines anymore.

OK, how do we figure this out?

The same way I figure anything else out: I create a mathematical image of the problem. There are many, many events which can be used to draw dividing lines across baseball history, some of them large and some of them small. These events include:

1) Rule Changes. The Designated Hitter Rule makes the game after 1973 different from the game before 1973.
2) Structural Changes. The split into divisions in 1969 makes

baseball post-1969 different from baseball pre-1969. Wild Cards and Interleague play are meaningful dividing lines in history.

3) Changes in the conditions of the game. Night baseball is a very important dividing line. Integration (Jackie Robinson) is an important dividing line. The banning of steroids is an important dividing line, and the arrival of steroids is a dividing event, although it is hard to find the start of it.

4) Changes in how the game is played. The 5-man pitching rotation (replacing the 4-man rotation) is a dividing line. The development of the modern closer is a dividing line.

5) Radical changes in statistical standards are dividing lines. The 1963-1968 era, when the pitchers dominated, is sort of a self-contained era, although this also can be marked off by rules changes. If I say "the stolen base era" you know what I mean by that—the Rickey Henderson/Vince Coleman/Tim Raines era.

6) Franchise moves are dividing lines. The move of the Dodgers and Giants to the coast (1958) is an important dividing line.

7) New ballparks are dividing lines, to an extent. The arrival of the Sterile Ashtray Stadiums (about 1970), the arrival of artificial turf, of domed stadiums...these things are dividing lines. The building of Camden Yards was a significant dividing line, because Camden Yards showed what modern ballparks could be with intelligence and imagination.

8) External events are dividing lines. World War II is a dividing line. 9-11 may be a dividing line (although I forgot to include it in my study, which I will report to you in a few minutes here.)

9) Players' careers are dividing lines. We speak of the 1920s as the Babe Ruth era, of the 1940s as the Joe DiMaggio era in New York, or the Ted Williams era in Boston, or the Stan Musial era in St. Louis. We speak of the 1950s as the Mickey Mantle/Willie Mays era.

10) Commissioners are dividing lines.

And there are probably others, which I may get to here or may not. Altogether I found 366 dividing lines or dividing events in baseball history—or more than that, depending on how you state things. I put the arrival of Ted Williams (1939) and the departure of Ted Williams (1960) on the same line, so I count them as one event, but that's actually two separate events.

Some of those events are more significant than others, obviously. I valued events at one through 10 points each, with the biggest and most obvious dividing lines counting as 10-point events. Most of the 366+ events were one-point events, and I had, altogether, 737 points worth of dividing lines separating 1871 from 2012.

Let's use the 1930s to illustrate the process. The All-Star Games begin in 1933. That's a dividing line; the "All-Star Era" begins in 1933. I counted that as a 2-point dividing line:

Year	Event	1930	1931	1932	1933	1934	1935	1936	1937	1938	1939	1940
1933	Beginning of All-Star Games	0	0	0	2	2	2	2	2	2	2	2

Every year after the All-Star games begin is different from every year before they began, so those 2 points carry forward to all future years, including 2012; those are 2 of the 737 points that separate 1871 from 2012.

The modern MVP Awards begin in 1931. That's a dividing line; I counted that as a 1-point event, making every year after 1931 "in" the MVP era, and every year before 1931 out of the era:

Year	Event	1930	1931	1932	1933	1934	1935	1936	1937	1938	1939	1940
1931	BBWAA MVP Awards	0	1	1	1	1	1	1	1	1	1	1
1933	Beginning of All-Star Games	0	0	0	2	2	2	2	2	2	2	2

The Hall of Fame opened in 1939; I counted that, again, as a two-point event:

Year	Event	1930	1931	1932	1933	1934	1935	1936	1937	1938	1939	1940
1931	BBWAA MVP Awards	0	1	1	1	1	1	1	1	1	1	1
1933	Beginning of All-Star Games	0	0	0	2	2	2	2	2	2	2	2
1939	Opening of Hall of Fame	0	0	0	0	0	0	0	0	0	2	2

The first night baseball game was played in 1935. Night baseball is a big deal in baseball history, a much more real and meaningful separator than the awards, but on the other hand, they didn't suddenly start playing a whole lot of night baseball in 1935. They started playing a whole lot of night baseball during World War II. I counted "night baseball" as a 7-point event, but put two of those points in 1935, when the first night game was played in the majors, and the other five in 1943. I'll add a totals line here:

Year	Event	1930	1931	1932	1933	1934	1935	1936	1937	1938	1939	1940
	Total of Dividing Events	0	1	1	3	3	5	5	5	5	7	7
1931	BBWAA MVP Awards	0	1	1	1	1	1	1	1	1	1	1
1933	Beginning of All-Star Games	0	0	0	2	2	2	2	2	2	2	2
1935	Beginning of Night Baseball	0	0	0	0	0	2	2	2	2	2	2
1939	Opening of Hall of Fame	0	0	0	0	0	0	0	0	0	2	2

1940 is separated from 1930, so far, by a total of 7 points. Bob Feller and Joe DiMaggio both reached the major leagues in 1936, Ted Williams in 1939:

Year	Event	1930	1931	1932	1933	1934	1935	1936	1937	1938	1939	1940
	Total of Dividing Events	0	1	1	3	3	5	7	7	7	10	10
1931	BBWAA MVP Awards	0	1	1	1	1	1	1	1	1	1	1
1933	Beginning of All-Star Games	0	0	0	2	2	2	2	2	2	2	2
1935	Beginning of Night Baseball	0	0	0	0	0	2	2	2	2	2	2
1936	Joe DiMaggio 1936-1951	0	0	0	0	0	0	1	1	1	1	1
1936	Bob Feller 1936-1956	0	0	0	0	0	0	1	1	1	1	1
1939	Opening of Hall of Fame	0	0	0	0	0	0	0	0	0	2	2
1939	Ted Williams 1939-1960	0	0	0	0	0	0	0	0	0	1	1

I started with a list of the 25 biggest superstars in baseball history, found a few other guys that I couldn't keep off the list, and wound up with I think 31 superstars whose arrival is a one-point dividing line in baseball history, and whose departure is another one-point dividing line. Everybody was one point, but I treated Babe Ruth different from anybody else, in that I also gave one point to Ruth's arrival in New York (1920) and one point to his departure from New York (1935), as well as a point for his departure from the game:

Year	Event	1930	1931	1932	1933	1934	1935	1936	1937	1938	1939	1940
	Total of Dividing Events	2	3	3	5	5	8	11	11	11	14	14
1914	Babe Ruth 1914-1935	1	1	1	1	1	1	2	2	2	2	2
1920	Babe Ruth in New York 1920-1934	1	1	1	1	1	1	1	1	1	1	1
1931	BBWAA MVP Awards	0	1	1	1	1	1	1	1	1	1	1
1933	Beginning of All-Star Games	0	0	0	2	2	2	2	2	2	2	2
1935	Beginning of Night Baseball	0	0	0	0	0	2	2	2	2	2	2
1936	Joe DiMaggio 1936-1951	0	0	0	0	0	0	1	1	1	1	1
1936	Bob Feller 1936-1956	0	0	0	0	0	0	1	1	1	1	1
1939	Opening of Hall of Fame	0	0	0	0	0	0	0	0	0	2	2
1939	Ted Williams 1939-1960	0	0	0	0	0	0	0	0	0	1	1

Eddie Collins and Pete Alexander also retired after the 1930 season and Rogers Hornsby played his last game in 1937 and Lou Gehrig in 1939, so there were also points for that, but...you understand the process, right? If you add in those four markers 1930 is at 6 and 1940 is a 22, a 16-point separation between those two years. We add one point for the turning of the calendar in 1940 (three points for the turning of the calendar in 1900 and 2000). John McGraw's retirement is a point.

There was only one ballpark added to the major leagues in the 1930s, Municipal Stadium in Cleveland (and it was only used for weekend games), but a new ballpark is a one-point event.

I marked off the decline in complete games in this way: on the line for "declining complete game percentage" I started at zero in 1871 and added 1 for each 5% decline in the percentage of games that were completed. In 1931, 48% of major league games were completed by the starting pitcher, so the score on that line is "10", meaning that we have crossed ten thresholds dividing baseball from the time when the starter almost always finished his work (starter completes less than 95% of games—1, starter completes less than 90% of games—2, starter completes less than 85% of games—3, etc.). In 1934 the percentage of complete games dropped to 43%, so that's an 11th marker in that column. There is a huge change in how the game is played; we have to construct a system that takes note of changes in how the game is played. This is one of the ways in which 2012 is very different from 1975.

One of the biggest changes in baseball in the 1930s was the organization of the minor leagues into farm systems. That happened between 1920 and 1940, mostly. It's a huge dividing line in baseball history—a 10-point divider, one of the big ones—but it did not happen all at once, so I counted that as 1 point in 1920, 1 point in 1922, 1 point in 1924, 1 point in 1926, etc., until the 10 points were all in in 1938.

The offensive norms changed. In 1931 (as best I can place it) the league-leading norm for hits dropped below 240 hits; that's a point. In 1931 the league-leading norm for triples dropped under 20. In 1933 the league-leading norm for batting average dropped under .380. In 1934 the league-leading norm for batter's strikeouts went over 100. In 1937 (as best I can place it) the league-leading norm for RBI dropped under 160. In 1939 the league-leading norm for runs scored dropped under 140, and the league-leading norm for hits dropped under 220. (It hasn't changed since 1939, by the way. It's been in the same "bracket"—200 hits to 220—since 1939, so there has been no point in that category since 1939.) In 1939 the league-leading norm for doubles dropped under 50. All of these things are separation points. (The league-leading norm for doubles dropped under 40 in 1970, but went back over 40 in 1973. The norm for a league-leading doubles total went over 50 in 1997, went back below 50 in 2009.)

If you add up all of the points separating 1930 from 1940, you have a total of 33 separation points. This is a very, very low total for a decade, one of the lowest ever. These are the point totals by decade since 1871:

1871	0		
1880	47	1871 to 1880	47 points
1890	123	1880 to 1890	76 points

1900	186	1890 to 1900	63 points
1910	253	1900 to 1910	67 points
1920	311	1910 to 1920	58 points
1930	357	1920 to 1930	46 points
1940	390	1930 to 1940	33 points

1950	432	1940 to 1950	42 points
1960	483	1950 to 1960	51 points
1970	569	1960 to 1970	86 points
1980	614	1970 to 1980	45 points
1990	646	1980 to 1990	32 points

2000	696	1990 to 2000	50 points
2010	729	2000 to 2010	33 points

The 1930s miss by only one point, in my system, of being the least "active" decade in baseball history, in terms of changes in the game. No separating line can reasonably be drawn through the 1930s, because there's just not much happening here—no rules changes, franchise shifts, strategic revolutions. There's the invention of the three major awards, the comings and goings of a good number of superstars, the beginning of night baseball, some changes in the statistical norms of the game, the gradual development of the farm systems, and one new ballpark; that's it.

The major dividing lines in baseball history, as I scored them, are:

- The re-formation of the National Association into the National League, 1876 (10 points),

- The gradual introduction of fielders gloves in the 1870s and 1880s (6 points),
- The switch of pitchers to pitching overhand from underhand, 1882-1883 (10 points),
  (Note: The changes in the ball and strike limits in this era are also extremely important, but since these rules were changed several times, there are several smaller point values for them, rather than one large immediate point total.)
- The collapse of the American Association, 1892 (6 points),
- The change to the modern pitching distance, 1893 (10 points),
- The contraction of the National League from 12 teams to 8, 1900 (6 points),
- The formation of the American League, 1901 (8 points),
- The beginning of the World Series, 1903 (8 points),
- The emergence of modern stadiums, dated 1908 (7 points),
- The banning of the corrupt players, 1920 (5 points),
- The banning of the spitball, 1920 (6 points),
- The arrival of the Commissioner system, 1921 (7 points),
- The Federal League ruling, 1921 (4 points),
- The beginning of baseball on radio, 1921 (5 points),
- The widespread use of night baseball, 1943 (5 points),
- The breaking of the color line, 1947 (7 points),
- The switch from travel by train to travel by airplane, 1952-1960 (5 points),
- The required use of batting helmets, 1956 (6 points, which seems now like about 3 points too many),
- The move of the Giants and Dodgers to the coast, 1958 (6 points),
- The first expansion and the switch from a 154- to a 162-game schedule, 1961-1962 (a total of 17 points for various things—2 points for each new team, 3 points for the expansion itself, 2 points for the move of the Twins to Minnesota, 2 points for the extra eight games on the schedule, 1 point for the new stadium in Washington.)
- The re-definition of the strike zone, 1963 (5 points),
- The institution of the amateur draft, 1965 (4 points),
- The second expansion in 1969 (8 points, 2 for each new team),
- The split into divisions in 1969 (5 points),
- The lowering of the mounds/restoration of the strike zone in 1969 (5 points),
- The DH Rule, 1973 (5 points),
- The Seitz decision granting free agency, 1977 (7 points),

• The switch from 4-man to 5-man starting rotations, 1976-1986 (6 points, gradual),
• The development of modern closers, 1978-1984 (6 points, gradual),
• The banning of steroids, 2005 (5 points).

The franchise shifts of the years 1953-1972 are also huge dividing lines, if taken aggregately, as are the aggregate changes in statistical standards which we account for one point at a time. The other expansions are all 4 points at a time (2 points per team), although with one of them there is an extra point or two for the Brewers moving to the National League. I gave 5 points every time the major league ERA moved from over 4.00 to under 4.00 (on a firm basis), or from over 3.00 to under 3.00. The major league ERA dropped under 4.00 in 2011, but we don't know yet if that's a firm change. If it is, that's a 5-point marker separating 2010 from 2011.

You are of course free to debate any of these choices, values or omissions as you see fit, and, if you know me at all, you know I'm not going to debate them with you. (I also posted my spreadsheet in which I did this accounting on Bill James Online so you can download it and study it at more length if you want to do that.)

OK, now we have a time line which measures changes in the game. Our next challenge is to use that time line to divide baseball history into eras.

Well, let me jump ahead to the conclusion. As a result of doing this work I now have a clear notion of where the dividing lines across baseball history should be drawn. The reason we do this, of course, is to enable us to think more clearly about the issue. By breaking the large, vague question (where are the dividing lines between baseball eras?) into a long series of small, specific questions which have definitively correct answers or answers requiring that we make a very small guess, we are able to create a much more focused picture of baseball's eras. These are the lines that I will advocate:

Era 1 (The Pioneer Era), 1871-1892
Era 2 (The Spitball Era), 1893-1919
Era 3 (The Landis Era), 1920-1946
Era 4 (The Baby Boomers Era), 1947-1968
Era 5 (The Artifical Turf Era), 1969-1992
Era 6 (The Camden Yards Era), 1993-2012

You can call them something else...you can call them the Cap Anson Era, the Ty Cobb/Honus Wagner Era, the Babe Ruth Era, the Willie Mays/Mickey Mantle Era, the Mike Schmidt Era, the Bud Selig Era. You can call them the Brickyard era, the Sharp Spikes Era, the Golden Era, the Jackie Robinson Era, the DH/Free Agent era, and the Steroid Era. You could call the last two eras the Labor Strife Era and the Labor Peace Era. I'll sell you the naming rights for $50.

Anyway, how did I arrive at these dividing lines, given what I have told you so far?

I tried about 40 different ways to break baseball history down into eras, and two of those ways worked better than the other 38; I'll skip the failures.

One of the two things that worked was, I planted a post every 25 years beginning in 1880—1880, 1905, 1930, 1955, 1980, 2005. By definition, there are going to be six eras in baseball history, and each will be about 25 years in length, more or less. Then I measured the changes in the game from the posts.

For example, I planted a post in 1930—assuming that the 1930 season would be in the center of an era—and I planted a post in 1955, assuming that the 1955 season would be in the center of an era. The question then becomes, where do we draw the dividing line between those two?

We start with simple math. The "Accumulated Change Score" in 1930 is 357; in 1955 it is 461. In 1940 the ACS score is 390, which is 33 points from 1930 but 71 points from 1955. Obviously, that goes in the era with 1930, rather than the era with 1955.

1941 is 41 points from 1930, but still 64 points from 1955.

1942 is 46 points from 1930, but 58 points from 1955.

1943 is 51 points from 1930, but 53 points from 1955.

1944 is the same, 51 and 53.

1945 is 53 points from 1930, but 51 points from 1955—so we COULD draw the dividing line between 1944 and 1945.

But that doesn't make sense, because there is only a two-point separation between 1944 (408) and 1945 (410). We can't draw a dividing line where there is no space.

1945 and 1946 is better; there is a five-point separation there based on the end of the war (3 points) and some other things. But still, 5 points is not a very large or satisfying separation.

There is an 11-point separation between 1946 and 1947 based on the breaking of the color line, the inauguration of the Rookie of the Year award, and some changes in statistical standards. I chose, then, to break between 1946 and 1947.

What we are doing, essentially, is asking ourselves "which is a more rational dividing line—the end of the war, or the end of segregation in baseball?" By working through this process we have narrowed our options down to those two, and it seems to me that the end of segregation in baseball is a better place to draw a line. That's what this is...a process of forcing ourselves to focus on the most relevant question.

The end of this era is the same thing; the 1968 season is actually a couple of points closer to 1980 than it is to 1955, but there is a 3-point separation between 1967 and 1968, and a 24-point separation between 1968 and 1969. Obviously, we draw the line where there is a 24-point separation, rather than a 3-point separation, so we end that era at 1968, and begin the new one in 1969.

The 1965 season has a surprisingly strong argument to be used as a dividing line. I did not anticipate this, since 1965 is in the middle of the 1963-1968 pitchers' epoch, and I would not be very willing to divide the eras in the center of a clearly identifiable period like that. But 1965 is

a) the beginning of the artificial turf era, and
b) the beginning of the amateur draft era.

Two fairly significant markers. Combining that with the election of a new Commissioner that year (Spike Eckert) and some other little stuff, 1965 makes a surprisingly good case to be considered the start of an era. But we rejected its appeal.

OK, so that system worked—the six pillars approach.

The second approach that worked was this. Suppose that we say that a new era begins whenever three standards are met:

1) At least ten years have passed since the commencement of the previous era,
2) The accumulated changes in the game since the commencement of the previous era total up to at least 100 points, and
3) There is a separation between two consecutive seasons of at least 10 points.

That method, it turns out, draws exactly the same lines as the six pillars approach....fudging just a little bit on one dividing line, but essentially it draws the same lines as the six pillars approach. The three markers of sufficient change approach has two other advantages: one, that it does not start with an *a priori* decision that there should be six eras each lasting about 25 years, thus cleans up one of the arbitrary elements of the process, and two, that it tells us where we are at the present time.

Using the six pillars approach, we can assume that we will transition into a new era sometime between now and 2030, but when? We really don't know where we are with respect to the era that we are in at the present time.

The three markers of sufficient change approach tells us that we are nearing the end of the Bud Selig era, nearing the end of the Camden Yards era, but that we are probably at least five years away from the next line. We are more than ten years into the era—mark one—and the accumulated changes in the game since 1993 total up to 74 points as I have scored them. I could have scored some of those differently; it is harder to get perspective on more recent events. I gave two points for the start of interleague play; maybe it should have been more. I gave no points for the All-Star game determining home field advantage in the World Series; maybe there should have been points for that. I gave 5 points for the banning of steroids in 2005; maybe it should have been 8. I gave no points for the major league ERA dropping under 4.00 in 2011, but I will if it stays under 4.00. Historical perspective requires time and distance.

But there will be changes next year. We re-aligned the divisions last year (2 points, probably), moving the Astros to the American League (1 point), plus we're probably selecting a new Commissioner within the next year or so (2 points). We have a new set of rules about the signing of amateurs taken in the draft; maybe I should have given a point for those. There are going to be very important new rules in the next few years reducing the salary discrepancies between rich teams and poor teams. It's hard to place a value on those rules until they are in place and we see what they do.

One more point, and then I'll shut up. Each era can be divided into epochs (or each epoch could also be divided into eras). I studied dictionaries, trying to figure out whether an "era" or an "epoch" was a larger event. It's not really clear; the definitions are fungible. I decided to use eras as larger periods and epochs as smaller).

Anyway, each era can generally be broken down into about five epochs, some clear and some fuzzy. The war years (1942-1945) are obviously an epoch within the Landis era. The pitching-dominated part of the 1960s (1963-1968) are obviously an epoch within the Baby Boomer era. The steroids "era" (1993-2005) was actually an epoch within the current era, the Camden Yards era.

In the second era in baseball history (1893-1919) there is a very important little "bubble" after the 1910 introduction of the cork-centered ball. We think of that era as the dead ball era. From 1906 through 1909 the league ERAs were around 2.50 every year, then the new "lively" ball, the cork-centered ball, was introduced, and for two or three years there were pretty big hitting numbers. Cobb and Joe Jackson hit over .400; runs scored were way up.

Then the scuff ball—invented in 1910—took over and spread around the league, and by 1915 the league ERAs were back to around 2.70. But there is a little epoch there, within the era, which is very different from the rest of the era, but it was so long ago, 100 years ago, that only the most fanatical baseball fans even know that this offensive boomlet ever occurred.

The issue of epochs within eras is an interesting one, but this article is too long to go into that now. Thanks for reading. I think we will be in a new era in baseball history by 2017.

———·—

(Post-season note, 2013.) There are several things that have happened since this article was first published in June, 2012, that have something of the feel of dividing lines. The re-emergence of the Pittsburgh Pirate franchise and the less dramatic but still notable success of the Kansas City Royals, the Pittsburgh Pirates of the American League, provide some evidence that the era in which small-market teams had little chance to compete may have hit, if not an end, at least an interruption. The re-emergence of the Pirates seems to me like a marker.

The new wild-card system, two wild cards in each league, is certainly a structural divide. The emergence of Mike Trout seems very likely to be a point making 2012 meaningfully different from 2011. Adding all of these together, I don't think we can conclude that we have entered a new era, but the changes separating us from 1993 are continuing to stack up.

———·—

CLASSICAL SPORT

by Bill James

My wife and I have season tickets to the symphony. I enjoy classical music, although, to be honest, this is my wife's thing that I do because she enjoys it, as she enjoys baseball games but going to baseball games is still my thing on some level.

Classical music has very, very serious problems as an industry. The number of people who enjoy classical music is small compared to the market for other kinds of music (Rock, Country, Rap, Jazz), and the market is composed primarily of old people. I'm 63; at classical concerts I am usually below the median age of the audience. Classical music is generally very expensive to produce, compared to other forms of music. We saw a Willie Nelson concert a few months ago; it's Willie Nelson, one of his daughters, and three or four other guys on a stage. We saw a symphony in the same hall last week; there is an 80- or 90-piece orchestra of very highly trained musicians, backed up by a choral group of 150 singers.

Classical music survives, or has survived so far, because it has advantages over the marketplace, rather than advantage *in* the marketplace. Classical music is perceived by a very large cadre of musical professionals as the highest form of music, and these people have integrated themselves and their music into the society in ways that insulate it from extinction by economic forces. High schools do not teach young musicians to play rock and roll, as a rule; they teach them to play "instruments," which are in truth the instruments of classical music. College music programs are 90% devoted to classical music. Music teachers teach small children to play simplified forms of Haydn and Chopin on the piano, rather than simple versions of Hank Williams and Little Richard. Millions of small children take violin lessons, which their parents get for them because this is how

23

music is taught. The perception that this form of music is "classy"—widely accepted in our culture—keeps the form alive by giving it these advantages, and many similar and related advantages. Governments fund classical music in dozens of ways that we would never consider funding rock and roll. Cities build concert halls designed for the symphony—and many or most cities help to fund their symphony orchestras. Government-sponsored radio plays hours a day of classical music, which is all but extinct on commercial radio.

At the Willie Nelson concert I am well above the median age and, I suspect, the median income. At the symphony I am below the median age and, I suspect, well below the median income. Those old people who go to the symphony have more-than-proportional power because they have more-than-proportional wealth. This is reflected in how the government spends its money.

There is something much more than that going on here. It has to do with the perception of rectitude, of value and of virtue. People who become symphony musicians are trained to do so from a very early age, are very, very highly trained, and go through layers of selection and rejection to reach that level. Rock musicians just pick up a guitar and start bangin'. "Trained" is the word I want to focus on.

On the spectrum of sport, baseball is toward the classical music end—and is becoming more so all the time. The Frisbee was invented in 1948 and became popular in the late 1950s. (Before that, we sailed can lids.) By the late 1960s we were playing Frisbee football. My son plays what he calls Ultimate Frisbee, which is just Frisbee football with a few wrinkles. His friends would never think to organize a baseball game or softball game among themselves. When they want to go out and run around a little, they play Frisbee football.

If we were to "train" very young boys to play Frisbee football, would that improve the sport? Should we make them take Frisbee football lessons when they are seven and eight? Should we buy them expensive equipment for Frisbee football? Should we put them on organized Frisbee football teams when they are very young, and demand that they produce birth certificates so that we can be sure no nine-year-olds are sneaking into the eight-year-olds league, and give them trophies, and take team pictures of them, and have the city pay someone to referee their Frisbee football games? Should we have parents who yell at their kids when the kids don't play Frisbee football *right*? Should we begin to pretend that Frisbee football is a test of character?

Well, if these things would not improve Frisbee football, why is it that people think that they are necessary and appropriate for baseball?

Music, like sport, is instinctive to us, exists in all cultures, and will never disappear. There are primal and sophisticated forms of music and of sport, which could also be called vibrant and calcified, or youthful and moribund. There is a spectrum in these activities that runs from vibrant, primal and youthful to sophisticated, calcified and moribund. All sports and all forms of music move across that spectrum, crawling toward obsolescence. Rock and roll has moved significantly to the right on that spectrum in the last 40 years; the very term "classic rock" suggests this. Football has lurched dramatically to the right.

But football and rock and roll are not as far advanced on this death march as is baseball. Baseball players, like symphony musicians, are fantastically highly trained, and they go through many layers of selection and rejection before they reach the highest levels. A baseball game is extremely expensive to stage. Even a youth baseball game now is relatively expensive to stage. Kids no longer perceive that they can play baseball in an empty lot with rocks and pieces of junk to mark the bases. Baseball now can only be played on manicured fields, which cities pay to maintain because youth baseball is perceived as a social good. The baseball audience is aging.

This is not a jeremiad. Baseball has massive resources and is in little danger of passing away in the next generation through calcification and decay. But neither does this represent a simple problem that can be addressed by advertising targeted at young people. Both baseball and classical music, for their own good, need to think deeply about how to re-energize themselves, how to make themselves younger, more vibrant, more accessible and less expensive

It's called hardening of the arteries. It kills us all sooner or later.

BIG GAME PITCHERS

by Bill James

———

Was Jack Morris, in fact, a Big Game Pitcher?

I will answer that question, eventually. I have done research that provides a clear and convincing answer to that question, but first there are quite a number of things that I have to explain, starting with this.

It is important for us not to be arrogant. Our field, I mean... sabermetrics, analytics, whatever you want to call it. It is important for us not to be trapped by the progression of the argument into thinking that we understand the issues better than we do.

And second, Jack Morris' credentials for the Hall of Fame are actually not half bad.

Jack Morris has become a Whipping Boy in the Hall of Fame debate, and this happened because of Bert Blyleven. I assume most of you know this, but...recapping quickly. People in our field tend not to put much weight on pitchers' won-lost records, and at least one of our crowd is campaigning to get rid of them entirely. Bert Blyleven has a strong Hall of Fame case in terms of Games Started, Innings, ERA, Strikeouts, Walks, Shutouts and analytical stats (and practical jokes; let's not forget the practical jokes.) Despite these assets, Blyleven was not elected to the Hall of Fame until 2011. He was not elected to the Hall of Fame until late in his eligibility largely because his won-lost record was not as good as his other stats. We sabermetricians don't much believe in won-lost records, so while he was Not Being Elected, Blyleven became the poster child of the analytics community.

As Blyleven became the favorite of our side of the debate, Jack Morris became the standard bearer for the Traditionalists. Morris has the opposite qualifications: fewer starts and innings pitched, a

27

higher Earned Run Average, many fewer strikeouts, more walks, and less than half as many shutouts. Morris pitched a thousand fewer innings than Blyleven, but still issued more walks. He does, however, own a better won-lost log than The Nasty Dutchman—33 fewer wins, but 64 fewer losses. Since Traditionalists believe in the Won-Lost records of pitchers, they believe in Jack Morris.

Or is it not quite that simple? Always dicey when you try to represent a set of views you don't actually believe in, but I'm sincerely trying. To Traditionalists, the argument can be boiled down to "Who do you want on the mound when you have to win a Big Game: Morris, or Blyleven?" Since Traditionalists advocate for Jack Morris, they thus advocate the position that Morris was a Big Game Pitcher. Morris did make 13 post-season starts and was 7-4 in the Post-Season (although even there his ERA was an unimpressive 3.80.) He pitched in three World Series, and won four games in those World Series, and of course he pitched a tremendous game in the 7th game of the 1991 World Series.

Of course, while Morris was 7-4 in post-season, Bert Blyleven was 5-1 with a much better ERA, 2.47, and while Morris led the Twins to a World Series championship in 1991, Blyleven did the same in 1987, so...that's not actually all that helpful, but back to Jack. According to Mike Ozanian in an article in Forbes, "I saw a ton of (Morris') games, as I did two hurlers who did get the nod for the Hall this year, Tom Glavine and Greg Maddux. Let me tell you something: if I to pick one of these three to win a game that my life depended on I would pick Morris in a heartbeat."

Well...I'd take Bret Saberhagen over any of those guys, too, but that doesn't necessarily mean he's a Hall of Famer. When he was on his game, Saberhagen was better than any of those guys including Morris, but I am trying to be conciliatory here, rather than argumentative. Ozanian casts the debate not as Analysts against Traditionalists, but as Winners against Fantasy-League Stats.

Morris credentials' for the Hall of Fame are not half bad. Let me make a Hall of Fame argument on his behalf:

1) While Won-Lost records of pitchers are often misleading for a single-season, they are also often instructive—and accurate. If you list the ten best starting pitchers in a league by Won-Lost records, and also by whatever analytical stat you prefer, they will sometimes be different, but normally six or eight of the ten are going to be the same guys.

2) A won-lost record is much more reliable as an indicator of the pitcher's ability over the course of a career than it is in

a single season. Over the course of a career, all of the things that trouble won-lost records in a season tend to become less of a problem.

3) Winning *is* the object of the game.

4) Historically, most pitchers who have career won-lost records similar to Jack Morris have been elected to the Hall of Fame. Morris was 254-186. If you take Red Ruffing, Burleigh Grimes, Jim Palmer, Eppa Rixey, Bob Feller, Ted Lyons, Red Faber, Carl Hubbell, Bob Gibson, Vic Willis, Amos Rusie, Herb Pennock, Three Finger Brown, Clark Griffith and Waite Hoyt, their won-lost records average 252-182, and all of them are in the Hall of Fame. If you throw Mordecai out of the group, their average record is actually 254-186, the same as Morris'.

5) Below that group of Morris comps there is another group of Hall of Fame pitchers whose won-lost records are distinctly LESS impressive than Morris'. Catfish Hunter, Jim Bunning, Rube Marquard, Dazzy Vance, Ed Walsh, Rube Waddell, Stan Coveleski, Chief Bender, Jesse Haines, Don Drysdale, Hal Newhouser, Bob Lemon.

6) If elected to the Hall of Fame, Morris would certainly not be the worst pitcher in there, although the same can also be said of many other pitchers such as Jim Kaat, Luis Tiant, Ron Guidry and Mike Mussina.

7) Morris' seven post-season wins are certainly a meaningful credential. What is the ratio of value, one post-season game to one regular-season game? Five to one? Ten to one? Twenty to one? Put enough value on the Post Season, and Morris goes over the line or, if you prefer to think of it that way, further over the line.

8) Pitching perhaps the greatest World Series 7th-game start of all time is not an insignificant accomplishment.

OK, but we circle back to the argument that Morris was a Big Game Pitcher, in general, rather than merely a Big Game Pitcher in the 1991 post-season. Traditionalists assert that Jack Morris was a Big Game Pitcher, because they have to assert this to defend Morris, and Analysts sneer and scoff at that because there is no general evidence for it, and also because sneering and scoffing are what we are best at.

We reject the argument that Jack Morris was a Big Game Pitcher because there is no evidence for it beyond a few World Series starts, but think about it. Is there any evidence that it *isn't* true? Have you ever seen any evidence that it isn't true? What if it *is* true?

This is what started me off on a two-week research tangent, neglecting my wife, my personal habits and the Boston Red Sox. What if it is true that Jack Morris was, in fact, a Big Game Pitcher? How would we know?

I am old enough to remember sabermetrics before some younger guys developed the concept of a leverage index, and one thing I remember is older analysts sneering at the value of relief pitchers, because the number of runs they save is small (relative to the number of runs saved by a starting pitcher.) What if there is a similar effect here: a Big GAME effect rather than a Big INNING effect, but we have not been seeing that because we have not been looking for it?

I decided to look.

What is a Big Game?
(skip this part if you don't care how I determine them)

To determine whether or not someone is a Big Game Pitcher, we have to begin by determining what is and what is not a Big Game.

I set up a point system to assign "Big Game Points" to every major league regular-season game played since 1952. Some of you who are more clever than I am with programming and certain types of calculations could approach this by figuring what each team's chance of reaching the World Series would be if they did win this game and what it would be if they didn't win this game, and then identify the biggest games by finding the games which have the biggest impact on a team's chance of reaching the World Series. That's a really complicated programming assignment, however, because you have to look at every other team in the league or the division to find the team with the best won-lost record, and then you have to look at every other team that could possibly beat you out for the Wild Card, etc.

If you can do that, I don't question but that your method would be better than my method, but I don't know how to do all of that, so I took a different approach. Every game starts with a base of 100 points, and the reason that every game starts with a base of 100 points is that if you don't give each game a base, then, using the approach I am using, you would reach the conclusion that games in September were like a hundred times more important than games in April. Games in September ARE much more likely to be "Big" games than games in April; in fact, in my system, there are no Big Games in April or May, but the value ratio isn't a hundred to one, either; it's more like four to one.

OK, so each game starts out at 100 basis points, and we increase that by one point for each game that goes off the schedule, so that the second game of the season is 101, the third game 102, the fourth game 103, etc.

Except that Big Games are for winners; if your team is 45-70 in August, then you're not going to play any Big Games, whereas if you are 70-45 and in a pennant race, then you will. So actually, we increase the game values by two points if a team wins a game, by one point if they lose, so that if your team is 45-70, then in Game 116 you have a Big Game Score of 260 (100 + 115 + 45), whereas if they are 70-45, then in Game 116 you have a Big Game Score of 285 (100 + 115 + 70).

We're just getting started. A game is a bigger game if you are playing a divisional opponent than if you are playing a team from the other division or the other league or a team from some other sport, so we add a 25-point bonus to each game played against a "direct" opponent. Prior to 1969 all games were played against direct opponents, because prior to 1969 there were no divisions and there was no inter-league or inter-species play, so prior to 1969 every game gets the 25-point bonus, whereas now, not so much.

A game is a bigger game when you are playing a good team than when you are playing a bad team; that is, from the Red Sox standpoint, it is a bigger game when we are playing the Yankees than when we are playing a last-place team, or, looking at it from the standpoint of the 2013 Arizona Diamondbacks, it is a bigger game when you are playing the Dodgers than when you are playing the Rockies. From the standpoint of the Cincinnati Reds, it is a bigger game when you are playing the Cardinals than when you are playing the Cubs, at least in 2013. I am sure 2014 will be all different.

Anyway, I initially factored this in by adding in the opposition's wins minus losses (based on their record so far this season), but it became apparent that this adjustment was too large. Suppose that your team has a record of 70-70, but the opposing team has a record of 90-50, and suppose it is a divisional opponent. The "Big Game Score", with that adjustment, would be 100 + 140 + 70 + 25 + 40, or 355.

But that adjustment turned out to be too large, because what that does is make it a Big Game if your opponent has a really good won-lost record, regardless of your own won-lost record. Think about it; if YOUR team was 90-50 and the other team was 70-70, the Big Game Score would be 335 (100 + 140 + 90 + 0). Because the OTHER team is 90-50, it goes up to 355. That's not right. At 90-50 you're not really 40 games over .500; you're 40 half-games over .500, so the appropriate adjustment is not 40 points, but 20. That way, when a 90-50 team plays a 70-70 team, you have a Big Game Score of 335 for each team.

Except that you wouldn't, ordinarily, because if your team was 70-70 and the other team was 90-50 and you were in the same division, it wouldn't be a Big Game at all, because you'd be dead. You would be virtually eliminated.

Ah, there's the rub. We discount games, and discount them sharply, after a team has been eliminated. After you've been eliminated, no game is a Big Game; it's just playing out the string. But this team hasn't been eliminated; they're merely dead as a doornail. If I allowed this to stand as a Big Game based on the fact that the 70-70 team has not been mathematically eliminated, the Big Game lists would be polluted by many, many games of teams which had no realistic chance of winning.

Here we hit a truly interesting question: When, exactly, is a team Virtually Eliminated? It is much like my somewhat famous little heuristic: The Lead is Safe. Same problem: where, exactly, do we draw the line between a team being in a difficult position, and virtually eliminated?

It is a truly interesting question which will lead us into some truly un-interesting math. I have written a formula to determine when a team has been Virtually Eliminated, and I will explain that formula to you in a moment, but first let me say this. *There is no right answer here.* There IS no exact moment at which a team is "virtually" eliminated. Is a team virtually eliminated when they are 5 games back with 5 to play, or not? I don't believe anybody has ever come back from that situation to win—but it certainly isn't impossible. If enough teams were exactly five games back with exactly five to play, sooner or later one of them would come back to win. Are you virtually eliminated if you are six and a half back with eight to play? Five and a half back? There is no right answer here.

We are flying in the face of Yogi Berra's most famous axiom: It ain't over 'til it's over. Saying that it ain't over 'til it's over is a totally unsatisfactory and totally unworkable answer from the standpoint of this particular problem, so we have to determine when it ain't over, but she's packed her bags and bought a bus ticket and called her momma. This is how we do that.

First, figure the team's Virtual Elimination Percentage; I'll explain how in a moment.

Second, figure the Schedule Completion Percentage; I'll explain how in two moments.

Third, if the Virtual Elimination Percentage, raised to the

power 1.8, is greater than the Schedule Completion Percentage, then the team is Virtually Eliminated.

The Virtual Elimination Percentage is figured as the highest win total in the division (or in the league, if you have no divisions in your league), plus the number of losses for the focus team, divided by three plus the number of scheduled games (which is 162 in modern baseball.) (If the number of losses for the focus team plus the number of wins for the first-place opponent exceeds 162, the team has been mathematically eliminated. The "+3" is put in this formula as a protection to ensure that we don't classify a team as Virtually Eliminated in the last four or five days of the season. In the closing days of the season, if you're not mathematically eliminated, then you have a realistic chance to win, no matter what.) Anyway, if your team is 70-70 and the first-place team is 90-50, then your Virtual Elimination Percentage is .9697, or 160 divided by 165.

The Schedule Completion Percentage is easy; that's just the percentage of your scheduled games (not including ties) that you have played. If you're 70-70 and scheduled to play 162 games, your Schedule Completion Percentage is .8642.

Raise the Virtual Elimination Percentage (.9697) to the power 1.8; you have .9461. That is greater than .8642, so...at 70-70, with another team at 90-50, you have been Virtually Eliminated.

Stick with me a minute. Suppose the first-place team is 90-50. If your team is 80-60, your Virtual Elimination Percentage is .9091; raise that to the power 1.80, you get .8424. That is LESS than the Schedule Completion Percentage, so your team has NOT been virtually eliminated. At 78-62, you haven't been Virtually Eliminated— but at 77-63, you have been. We have to draw a line somewhere; that's where we draw it. 13 games out with 22 to play, you're dead.

I intended for this to work out so that we could use the SQUARE of the Virtual Elimination Percentage, rather than raising it to the power 1.80, but...raising it to the square turned out to be just too damned tolerant, too lenient. (Thanks, Obama.) Using the square, rather than the power 1.80, a team was not virtually eliminated if they were 77-63 when another team was 90-50. My judgment is that, in that situation, you ARE virtually eliminated. 77-63 against 90-50...you're absolutely not winning.

Actually, raising it to the power 1.80 is too tolerant, too. 1.60 or 1.70 would probably be more realistic, but I wanted to err on the side of caution. I do not want to declare a team dead as long as they could still rally and win, even if it would take a miracle. But—and this is a tremendously key point, so I'm going to repeat this phrase about four times—when you err on the side of caution, it is still an error. *When you err on the side of caution, it is still an error.* I am not looking to declare a team "dead" if they are not COMPLETELY dead. A doctor in an emergency room will continue to work on a trauma victim, knowing full well that the patient is dead, because *there is no percentage in declaring him dead when he might somehow, conceivably, still be brought back to life.* When declaring someone dead, you always err on the side of caution. Same here; when declaring a team dead, we err on the side of caution—BUT WHEN YOU ERR ON THE SIDE OF CAUTION, IT IS STILL AN ERROR.

The importance of this is to acknowledge that our system is not perfect, and to declare, furthermore, that it cannot be made perfect. A system of this nature will always contain error. But I'm mirroring the way that real teams think about this. I will tell you this: that in 2004, when the Red Sox were down to the Yankees three games to none in the playoffs and had just been humiliated 19-8, we met back in the bowels of Fenway Park, where an important person in the Red Sox system said, "We have to look at it like we are still going to win this thing, like we are going to go out and win the next four games. Of course we know it won't happen, but that is how we HAVE to look at it." And...son of a bitch, they did it. In real life, you never concede defeat until there is just no conceivable way you can come back and win it. So...I don't declare a team Virtually Eliminated until there is just no conceivable way they can come back and win it.

But this policy causes us to include in the list of Big Games a certain number of games by teams which have, in fact, only the slightest chance of winning. We discount a team's Big Game Score, after the team is Virtually Eliminated, so that no game by a team which has been Virtually Eliminated will be included in the Big Game lists.

Small note...sometimes the math is screwy in the opening days, so there is a codicil in the procedure that says that no team is Virtually Eliminated until they have lost at least 40 games. Also, there is a rule in the system that says that if your won-lost record is 0-0 (Opening Day), add 100 points to the Big Game Score. Because of that, the Big Game Score for Opening Day is 200, or, since teams are normally playing in-division on Opening Day, normally 225. This has nothing really to do with the study, since 225 isn't a big enough number to designate the afternoon's amusement as a Big Game, but it does mean that on a bad team that is virtually eliminated in June, their biggest game of the season is Opening Day. I put that rule in because it is realistic, but it doesn't have anything to do with the study.

But I still had a problem, at this point, which was that I had too many games being listed as Big Games by teams that were not

Virtually Eliminated, but which could not honestly be said to be in a pennant race. A team is 60-65 in late August and 15 games behind; under the right circumstances, it can show up as Big Game, which is not right because if you are 15 games behind in late August, it is not a Big Game. I had to put in an "Early Elimination Penalty".

What is the Early Elimination Penalty? Well, if

a) A team has lost at least 40 games,
b) Their "Virtual Elimination Percentage" exceeds their Schedule Completion Percentage by at least .2000, and
c) That team also has no chance at a Wild Card,

Then we apply an Early Elimination Penalty, which has the effect of removing that team's games from the Big Game list.

With, however, two more obscure and annoying provisos—

1) That we don't apply the Early Elimination Penalty to any team with a winning record before the first of September, and
2) That we don't apply the Early Elimination Penalty to any team with a winning record in the Wild Card era, even in September.

All of that sounds complicated and obscure, and it is—but even with all of those outs and exclusions, the Early Elimination Discount is applied to 42,751 games in our study, so...it's not like it's a trivial adjustment. It is a necessary adjustment to prevent the Big Game List from being polluted by teams that couldn't find a pennant race with a bloodhound, even though they have not been either mathematically eliminated or virtually eliminated.

When you get through all of that, of course, you have to figure out whether a team has been not merely Eliminated or Virtually Eliminated, but also whether they are still in the hunt for a Wild Card. And when we have done all of that and eliminated all of the teams which need to be eliminated, we will have a Big Game Score for every team in every game of every season.

Regular Season Big Games

We are dealing here only with regular season games. Let us assume that all post-season games are designated as Big Games; what we are asking is which regular-season games should also be similarly designated.

The biggest game in my data, by this system, is the third game of the 1962 National League playoff series between the Dodgers and the Giants—the 165th game of a 162-game season. Johnny Podres started against Juan Marichal; the Giants won. That game scores at 411 for each team. The second-biggest score in our system in the same series the previous day, Drysdale against Jack Sanford, and the third-biggest is the first game of that series.

Next on the list is the Bucky Dent game at Fenway Park, October 2, 1978. After that we have a Cardinals/Mets game at the end of the 1985 season, then a Blue Jays/Yankees game, also at the end of the 1985 season. The top 100 or so include all of the play-in games for races that have ended in a tie. In the top 100 games there is no game that occurred earlier on the calendar than September 25, and the biggest of Big Games are always games between two teams with excellent won-lost records.

In the way that I have stated this so far, you might assume that every game which appears on the Big Games list for one team must also appear on the list for the other, but that isn't true. Sometimes a game can be huge for one team, but completely meaningless for the other. In general, of course, a Big Game for one team is also a Big Game for the other team, but not always and absolutely, so when I say "the 100 biggest games in the data" or something like that, what I mean is the 100 biggest for one team. You're probably talking about 55 different games there, with 45 of them used twice.

Big games tend to occur

• Late in the season,
• Between two good teams,
• Who are going head to head in their division.

But we're generalizing. Sometimes it is two good teams which are not in the same division, but they still need a win. Sometimes it is a really good team playing a not-so-good team, but it is the last week of the season and one team or the other really needs a win. And remember; our answer isn't necessarily a perfect answer; it is merely the best answer that I can give you.

The next question we have to ask is, "What is the cutoff to be counted in our study as a Big Game?" The answer to that one is "a Big Game Score of 310 or higher", and the answer to the follow-up question "why?" is "because I said so."

Again, there is no compelling logic on that little issue; we just have to choose what seems most reasonable. At 310, we have 7.7% of all major league games in the data designated as "Big Games", or one game in 13. If we were to use 300 as the cutoff, rather than 310, then we would have almost exactly 10% of the games designated as Big Games. That would be a satisfying confluence of two round numbers—300, and 10%—so it is tempting to say that 10% of all games are Big Games, and be done with it.

The problem is, it just doesn't feel right. When we use the term "Big Games" we have to try, as best we can, to match our definition to the way that an ordinary sportswriter would ordinarily use the term; in other words, we have to try to get a list of Big Games that an unbiased observer would agree are Big Games. At 300 (10%), we're just a little bit short of that.

Here's what you have at "300"—and there are more than 600 games in the data that score at exactly 300, but picking a few of them at random to illustrate the problem.

On September 2, 2011, the Angels played the Twins in Anaheim, Tyler Chatwood opposing Carl Pavano. The Angels came into the game 74-63, three and a half games out of first place, behind the Rangers. The Twins—NOT in the same division—were 57-79 and Virtually Eliminated, so it was not a Big Game for them; it scored at 300 for the Angels.

Big Game? Well…you can say it is a Big Game (for the Angels) if you want to. From my standpoint, it just isn't *quite* enough. Every game, even in September, isn't a Big Game. A week later, the Angels still three and half back, that would be a Big Game. If they were playing a division opponent, that would be a Big Game; if they were playing a stronger team in another division, that would be a Big Game. It's just not quite enough that, in my judgment, an ordinary observer would tend to mention that as a Big Game.

August 6, 1971, Red Sox playing the Tigers in Fenway Park. The Red Sox are in second place, 63-46. The Tigers—in the same division at that time—are in third place, 58-52, but still 10 games behind the Baltimore Orioles. The game scores at 300 for the Red Sox, and 301 for the Tigers. Ray Culp pitches against Joe Coleman.

Big Game? Again, you can say it is a Big Game if you want to. I wouldn't suggest that you were wrong. It is certainly much bigger than the average game. It is bigger than 90% of the games on the schedule of an average team. It's a pennant race, it's August, two good teams…it is not unreasonable to say that it is a Big Game.

But in my judgment, it is just not quite big enough. Late August, the same teams, OK. If the teams are 80-59 and 79-61 rather than 76-62 and 73-66, and thus a little bit closer to first place, OK, that's a big game. But I just don't think an ordinary observer is going to remember that one as a Big Game.

Third example: August 23, 1985, at Shea Stadium, the Padres against the Mets. A Friday night. The Padres come in at 66-55, in second place in the NL West, six and a half games behind the Dodgers. The Mets are at 73-47, in second place, a game behind the Cardinals. Sid Fernandez against somebody named Roy Lee Jackson.

A Big Game? Enn...it's not a *Little Game* certainly. It's late August; first place is on the line for the Mets. The Padres are very much in the race. It's bigger than 90% of random games. But in my judgment, it's just not quite enough to say that that's a Big Game, if what we mean by that is "These are the games by which pitchers are going to be judged."

If you set the cutoff at 320 you have the opposite problem. At 300 you're including games you should not include; at 320 you are excluding games that you probably SHOULD include. So...at 310 we have 7.7% of all games included, and I've drawn the line at 310 Big Game Points.

It's a "hard" 310, by the way; 309.5 is NOT a Big Game. In the data there are 241,536 Game Lines—almost a quarter of a million— of which 18,530 starts are designated by this process as Big Games. Now we'll start naming names as to who was and who wasn't a Big Game Pitcher.

Best Regular-Season Big Game Pitchers Since 1952

OK, who would you guess pitched the most Big Games in his career, regular season, within this data?

It is not a surprise. It is the same guy who made the most post-season starts. Andy Pettitte. In his 18-year major league career, Pettitte made 82 regular-season starts which are designated by our system as Big Games. This broke by one the previous record of 81, which was shared by Jim Palmer and Roger Clemens.

The data for Pettitte and Palmer almost matches. Palmer made 521 starts in his major league career, of which 81 were Big Games. Pettitte also made 521 starts, of which 82 were Big Games. Clemens made many more career starts than Pettitte and Palmer, but he also started 81 Big Games.

No one can be surprised by this data. Palmer's Orioles were in contention almost every year of his career...maybe literally every year, I don't know. Palmer started Big Games for the Orioles in 1966, 1969, 1970, 1971, 1972, 1973, 1974, 1975, 1976, 1977, 1978, 1979, 1980, 1982 and 1983. An ordinary pitcher could never do that because most teams don't play Big Games every year. Most teams aren't in contention every year. The Orioles in that era were.

These are the ten pitchers who started the most Big Games in regular season, according to my system and within my data:

Rank	First	Last	Big Games
1	Andy	Pettitte	82
2	Jim	Palmer	81
3	Roger	Clemens	81
4	Don	Drysdale	79
5	Steve	Carlton	76
6	Don	Sutton	76
7	Johnny	Podres	74
8	Whitey	Ford	73
9	Juan	Marichal	71
10	Sandy	Koufax	70

Ties broken by percentages; Palmer ranks ahead of Clemens because his percentage was higher. We are missing thirteen starts from Whitey Ford's career here because we start the data after the 1952 season, so his total would be a little bit higher, although it would not be high enough to beat Pettitte.

As a percentage of starts, the 1 and 2 guys are longtime teammates, almost career teammates, Koufax and Podres. The Dodgers in that era played a tremendous number of Big Games. The Dodgers were in close pennant races in 1954, 1956 (one game), 1959 (playoff with Milwaukee), 1961, 1962 (playoff with San Francisco), 1963, 1965 and 1966. It led to a large number of Big Games—the highest percentages ever.

Number three on the "percentage" list, though, is a current guy: Jon Lester. Lester has made 220 starts so far in his career, 41 of them Big Games. Again...not a surprise to anybody in Boston.

Much of that list (highest percentages) is composed of surprising names, and I'll get back to that in a moment. Let's run the "most Big Games, career" list out to 25 or 26 or 27:

Rank	First	Last	Big Games
11	Jerry	Reuss	70
12	Greg	Maddux	69
13	David	Wells	68
14	Jimmy	Key	67
15	Gaylord	Perry	66
16	Tom	Glavine	62
17	CC	Sabathia	61
18	Tim	Wakefield	60
19	Doyle	Alexander	60

Rank	First	Last	Big Games
20	Tommy	John	60
21	Pedro	Martinez	59
22	Roy	Oswalt	58
23	Milt	Pappas	58
24	John	Lackey	57
25	Tim	Hudson	57
26	Bob	Gibson	57
27	Tom	Seaver	57

The first guy on the list that you might not have expected to see there is Jerry Reuss, who started 70 Big Games. Reuss spent most of his career with the Pirates (1974-1978) and the Dodgers (1979-1987)—both perennial contenders, and Reuss did win 220 games in his career, although he failed somehow to become a household name. Roy Oswalt, John Lackey and Tim Hudson are contemporary guys who have made a lot of Big Game starts.

Back to the percentage list. Behind Koufax, Podres and Jon Lester on the "percentage of career starts which were Big Games" list are:

4. Joey Jay. Wouldn't have thought of him, would you? Jay came up with the Braves in the 1950s. They were always in contention, although Jay was never able to establish himself there—no fault of his, actually. He always pitched well for the Braves, but they had Spahn, Burdette and Buhl, and they didn't trust anybody else.

Anyway, traded to Cincinnati in 1961, Jay went 21-10 for the Reds, leading them to the National League pennant, then won 21 games again in 1962, for a team that went 98-64. The Reds stayed competitive in 1963 (86-76), 1964 (92-70), and 1965 (89-73); then Jay was finished, so he never pitched much for a non-competitive team.

5. Jim O'Toole. Same team, Reds of the early 1960s.

6. Stan Williams. A teammate of Koufax and Podres.

7. John Lackey. A teammate of Jon Lester. We are seeing a pattern here.

8. Bruce Kison. Pirates of the 1970s, Angels of the 1980s, and, as we will see, very much a Big Game Pitcher although he was not a rotation workhorse like most of these other guys.

9. Jimmy Key. Blue Jays of the 1980s and early 1990s, Yankees of the later 1990s.

10. Whitey Ford.

On the other side of the ledger:

Zach Duke, 169 starts, mostly for the Pirates of the last decade...never started a Big Game. Actually, there are many, many pitchers in our data who never started a Big Game; there are lots of pitchers who work in rotation for two or three years, bad team...they never start a Big Game. Duke made more starts than anyone else, though, who completely missed the opportunity to start a Big One. Other pitchers who never started a Big Game: Bob Bruce (Astros of the 1960s), Pete Broberg, Turk Farrell, Steve Arlin, Dave Lemanczyk.

More notable than any of those, though, is Randy Jones, Padres of the 1970s, a 20-game winner in 1975 and 1976, and the National League Cy Young Award Winner in 1976. Jones—many of you will remember him—was a lefty who was a ground ball machine, didn't throw hard. Jones made 285 major league starts—one Big Game, by our standards. September 6, 1978, the Padres were 71-68, in fourth place, eleven and a half out but still alive. The Padres were in Atlanta that day, Jones started against Mickey Mahler, and the Padres won the game, 5-3. But they lost 4 out of the next 5, dropped out of contention. That was the one and only Big Game start of Randy Jones' career.

Jack Morris? Yeah, he pitched some Big Games. Morris made 46 Big Game starts in his career, which is 58th on our list, and is an above-average percentage (8.7%). Bert Blyleven made 47 Big Game starts, which is a below-average percentage (6.9%). Koufax and Podres pitched Big Games in 22% of their career starts; Jon Lester, in 19% so far. 7 to 9% is not a notable number, one way or the other.

Who was and who wasn't a Big Game Pitcher?

So who was a Big Game Pitcher, and who really wasn't? Before I get into that, let me say this: that it is most satisfying, from my standpoint, to find a new way to make distinctions among pitchers which is both valid and meaningful. I do a lot of studies, looking at this effect or that effect, in which, at the end of a couple of weeks of study, everybody comes out about the same. Not true here. Andy Pettitte made 82 Big Game starts in his career; Randy Jones made 1. Frank Tanana made almost a hundred more starts in his career than Andy Pettitte, but made only 35 Big Game starts. The data makes real and sizeable distinctions.

And second, no one reasonably could doubt that these are valid distinctions. They confirm in hard facts a lot of what we knew intuitively before—that Jon Lester has made a lot of Big Game starts in his career, that Mark Langston made very few, that Ben Sheets made very few but that James Shields has made a lot. No one can doubt that these things are true, I don't think.

As to the performance differences...those you can question whether they are meaningful or not. In a moment I will tell you about a pitcher who was not well respected, who was always thought of as kind of a flake, but who went 17-6 with a 2.67 ERA in his career in Big Games, whereas there is another pitcher, a bigger name pitcher, who went 5-19 with a 4.04 ERA. Is this predictive information?

Who knows? I'm not claiming it is. Thus far in his career, Cole Hamels is 14-6 with a 2.59 ERA in Big Games; Matt Garza is 6-13 with a 4.79 ERA (in regular season.) If they meet in a Big Game this year, that doesn't mean Hamels will win.

But what happens in Big Games is important whether or not it is indicative of an underlying skill. Bill Mazeroski's home run in the 1960 World Series is a big deal, whether or not it had anything to do with Mazeroski's ability as a hitter. Madison Bumgarner pitching 8 shutout innings in the 2010 World Series and 7 shutout innings in the 2012 World Series is important, whether or not it has anything to do with Bumgarner's character, his underlying skills, or the allegation that he has a girl's first name and is a bad gardener.

At risk of offending 70% of you to illustrate the point...Lee Harvey Oswald is historically important, whether or not he was a good shot with a rifle. Underlying skills are not always the issue; sometimes the issue is simply what he did. Underlying skills are important in the winter, when you are putting together next year's team—but when you are looking back at last year's team, what matters is performance, not ability.

1. A Bunch of Guys who Have About the Records You Would Expect In Big Games

Jim Palmer, who shared the record for Regular Season Big Game Starts until September of 2013, was 36-26 with a 2.72 ERA in Big Games...probably about the record you would expect. Your won-lost record tends to flatten out in Big Games, because you're almost always facing a strong opponent. **Roger Clemens** was 41-25 in Big Games, 3.70 ERA...you might have expected the ERA to be a little better. **Jerry Reuss** was 26-21, 3.34.

Greg Maddux made 69 Big Game Starts in his career; he was 35-21, 2.98 ERA. That's probably about what you would expect from Maddux. **John Smoltz** was 18-13, 3.29: I guess you might have expected him to do even better, given his 15-4 won-lost log in post-season play. Ferguson Jenkins was 26-19, 3.24. **Mike Torrez** was 20-16, 3.22; **Mark Buehrle** is 18-16, 4.26. **Vida Blue** was 21-16, 3.41. **Kenny Rogers** was 21-14, 3.53, and **Ken Holtzman** was 19-19, 3.38. **Bartolo Colon** is 20-13 in Big Games, 3.47 ERA.

Tom Seaver in Big Games was 30-17, 2.84 ERA; you're probably not surprised at that. **Dave Stieb** had a good 3.05 ERA in Big Games, but was just 14-14...consistent with his career. **Jack Sanford** was the opposite, 17-8 but with a 4.22 ERA. **Jim Bunning** was 17-13, 3.31. **Claude Osteen** was 14-21 in Big Games, 4.18 ERA. **Catfish Hunter** was 20-13, 3.21 ERA; **Jerry Koosman** was about the same, 18-12, 3.20. **Esteban Loaiza** is 15-17, 4.92 ERA; that's not good, but then, I'm guessing you wouldn't have expected him to be great. **Dan Haren** is 15-20 in regular season Big Games, 4.13 ERA; **Ervin Santana** is 13-14, 3.71. **Big Game James Shields** is 18-12, 3.44. **Lew Burdette** was 16-10, 3.73; we're missing a few starts from him, because my data from the 1950s isn't complete. **Joey Jay**, who made a high percentage of Big Game starts, was 15-14, 3.77 ERA. **Jim Lonborg** was 16 and 13, 3.55.

Don Larsen, famous for his one Big Game, was 12-4 in regular season Big Games, 3.25 ERA; you're probably not surprised at that. **Sal Maglie** in the data we have was 11-3 with a 2.54. Sal was known as The Barber because he liked to give the hitters a close shave. He was famous as a Big Game Pitcher. In 1956 he went 13-5 for Brooklyn but, rather remarkably, finished second in the MVP voting, because he was perceived as the player who had won the Big Games.

In the 1970s, **Larry Gura** was kind of the Royals' Big Game Pitcher. Gura knocked around as an extra man until he was almost 30 years old. In 1976, with the Royals, he was still in that role, just an extra guy, but he was pitching zeroes out of the bullpen late in the season. He had cut his ERA from 3.57 on September 1 down to 2.79 on September 28, had not given up a run in September, when Whitey Herzog decided to start him at Oakland on September 29. Huge, huge game; Big Game Score of 380. Oakland had won the division five straight years, three World Championships. Kansas City had lost four games in a row, blowing more than half of a six-game lead. They were clinging to a two and a half game lead with four games left; KC was 89-69, Oakland was 86-71.

Gura had made only one start all season, and had not even been a regular part of the bullpen most of the year; he was an up-and-down guy, what we call now a 4A player. Gura threw a 4-hit shutout, effectively ending the pennant race. After a couple of more Big Games he became Herzog's Big Game guy. He made 30 Big Game starts in his career, a high percentage; he was 14-10 with a

3.04 ERA. **Splittorff** was 14-16, 4.61; **Dennis Leonard** was 19-13, 3.56. Leonard threw a bunch of shutouts in Big Games.

Sudden Sam McDowell was just 5-10 in Big Games, but had a good 2.79 ERA. **Orel Hershiser** was 14-6, 2.90. **Ted Lilly** is 13-10 in Big Games, 3.57 ERA; **Tim Lincecum** is 14-9, 2.59. **Mickey Lolich** was 23-16, 2.96; **Denny McLain** was 10-9, 3.63. **Gil Meche** made only 7 Big Game starts in his career; he was 1-4 with a 7.99 ERA. **Kevin Millwood** was 17-14, 3.73. **Jamie Moyer** was 23-17, 3.48. **Joe Niekro** was better than **Phil** in Big Games; Joe was 16-14, 3.38 ERA; Phil was 16-15, 3.71. Phil pitched very few Big Games in his best years, with Atlanta; most of his Big Game starts came in 1969 and in the early 1980s, when he was past 40 years old.

Camilo Pascual came up with the Senators in 1954, but never pitched a Big Game until 1960. In the 1960s he made 21 Big Game starts, going 9-9 with a 3.49 ERA.

2. Some Guys Who Were Better Than You Would Expect

Jim Rooker was a minor league outfielder for several years. In 1962, in the low minors, he hit .281 with 16 homers, 80 RBI, also 27 stolen bases in 31 attempts. He followed that up with .272 at Duluth the next season, 19 homers, but as he moved up the line he stopped hitting and stopped getting promoted. After a couple of years he switched to the mound.

He made slow but steady progress as a pitcher, and was taken by the Kansas City Royals in the 1969 expansion draft (the draft, actually, was October of 1968; the expansion was in 1969.) With the expansion Royals in 1969 he was 4 and 16 on the mound, but had a tremendous season at bat, hitting .281 with 4 homers, slugging over .500.

After four years in Kansas City he was traded to Pittsburgh. He found pitching for a good team much more to his liking. He made 37 Big Game starts in his career, and was 21-9 with a 2.38 ERA.

Mike Hampton was 15-11 in Big Games, 2.49 ERA. **Clay Buchholz** so far in his career has been 9-4 in regular season Big Games, 15 starts, with a 1.98 ERA...one of the best in the data. **Mark Prior** was 10-1 with a 2.06 ERA, and struck out 132 batters in 109 innings. **Cal Eldred**, who was 11-2 with Milwaukee in 1992 and 10-2 with the White Sox in 2000, also went 9-1 in his career in Big Games, 2.23 ERA.

Gary Peters, early 1960s, had a 2.24 career ERA in 37 Big Game starts, one of the best ERAs in the data for a pitcher with 25 or more starts, although his won-lost record was just 17-12. **Joel**

Horlen, his teammate, was just 11-13, but with a 2.26 ERA. The White Sox under Eddie Stanky, mid-1960s, used to store the baseballs in a refrigerator so that they would be damp and dead, negating the other team's power; I believe this was one of the reasons the leagues assumed the responsibility for taking care of the baseballs to be used in the games. Anyway, in 1967 the American League batting average was .236, and the Park Factor in Chicago was .81, so there were not a lot of runs scored there. Peters was like Rooker, though; he was a lefty who could hit homers.

Wally Bunker, who won 19 games as a 19-year-old in 1964, then had arm troubles the rest of his career, was 11-2 in Big Games, 2.37 ERA. **Bill Stafford**, same era, essentially the same story but not quite, was 10-2, 2.43. Stafford was in the Yankees' starting rotation in 1961 at the age of 21, with little minor league experience, and pitched well; that was common in that era. There were a lot of 19-, 20-, 21-, 22-year-old pitchers in that era. **Ray Sadecki** was another one—a rotation starter for the Cardinals in 1959 at the age of 19. He also was good in Big Games—22 wins, 12 losses, 3.35 ERA.

It is surprising that so many of these peach fuzz pitchers from that era had outstanding records in Big Games. **Jack Fisher** was another—in the rotation for the Baltimore Orioles in 1961 at the age of 21, later had some horrible won-lost records with the Mets in the mid-1960s, losing 24 games for them in 1965. He was 11-3 in Big Games, 3.41 ERA; that's mostly based on his work with Baltimore. He didn't pitch any Big Games for the Mets.

Earl Wilson was famous for a no-hitter in Fenway Park in 1962, the first black pitcher to pitch a no-hitter in the American League. He homered in that game; he hit 35 homers in his career, which is near the record for a pitcher. Wilson won 22 games for the Tigers in 1967. He was 13-6 in Big Games, 2.79 ERA. **Wade Miller** has been 10-3, 2.38.

Ed Figueroa, Yankees of the 1970s, was 13-4 in Big Games, 2.61 ERA; I didn't know that. **Charlie Hough** was 13-5, 2.73—the only knuckleball pitcher who was effective in Big Games. **Nelson Briles**, a fourth starter much of his career behind guys like Gibson and Carlton, was 13-7, 2.61 ERA.

Doyle Alexander was 29-18 in Big Games, 3.72 ERA; that's kind of a surprise. Doyle Alexander won 194 games in his career, but never had a big season, didn't throw hard, and was a baseball nomad, bouncing from team to team and not leaving too many friends behind him. But he pitched sensationally well for the Tigers down the stretch in 1987 (9-0), and that is where a good part of his Big Game resume comes from.

OK, here's a big surprise. **Jim Kaat** won 283 games in his major league career, won 25 games in 1966, won 20 games in 1974 and 1975, but he isn't in the Hall of Fame, in large part because he wasn't perceived as a Big Game Pitcher. In fact, his record in Big Games is great. That turns into a long-winded digression, so I made it a separate section below.

3. Some Guys Who Were Not as Good in Big Games as You Might Expect

Nolan Ryan was 20-21 in Big Games, 3.68 ERA. **Tommy John** was 21-21, 4.06. Ryan and John are the most perfect polar opposites in the pitching world—a right-hander versus a lefty, the ultimate power pitcher versus the ultimate ground ball pitcher. They were alike in this respect...their records in Big Games were about the same.

Josh Beckett, who always carried the reputation of being a Big Game monster, is actually 19-22 in Big Games, 4.22 ERA. **David Cone** was just 15-19, 3.88 ERA, although he struck out 292 batters in 304 innings. David Cone and Bret Saberhagen were the same age and signed with the Royals about the same time. Both have similar records (194-126 for Cone, 167-117 for Saberhagen), but Saberhagen was far, far better in Big Games.

Livan Hernandez, MVP of the 1997 World Series, was just 13-14 in Big Games in regular season, 4.26 ERA. **David Wells** was just 24-26 in Big Games, 4.75. He was 239-157 overall, so that's 215-131 when it isn't a Big Game (.621), but under .500 in Big Games.

Sandy Koufax was just 28-26 in Big Games, but that's kind of misleading, so I don't want to dwell on it. Well...it is kind of a shocking fact. Koufax' career record was 165-87, so that means he was 137-61 when he wasn't a Big Game (.692), but 28-26 when it was (.519). He lost Big Games whenever he had to pitch one in the 1950s, and also a few in 1962, when he tried unsuccessfully to come back from his medical problem at the end of the season, without doing a proper rehab. But there are different ways of looking at the question of how effective a pitcher was in Big Games, and in Koufax' case those other ways of looking at the issue get different answers, so I don't want to mislead you. 98 times in 100, the other ways of looking at the issue just tell you the same thing with different numbers, so we can ignore them, but in Koufax' case we need to look at more data, which I'll explain later.

Pedro Martinez' record in Big Games was not great, either (25-22, 3.34 ERA. He did strike out 424 batters in 371 innings.) Red

Sox fans will remember that Pedro had a stretch of about three years when he just couldn't beat the Yankees. His record in Big Games OTHER than the Yankees was good, but the four biggest regular-season games that Pedro pitched were all against the Yankees, and the Red Sox lost all four of them.

4. One Pitcher to Whom I Owe an Apology

Don Drysdale. In *The Politics of Glory* (1994, I think), I studied Don Drysdale's record in Big Games, and concluded that it was poor. Drysdale died suddenly just before that book came out, so the claim that Drysdale had a poor record in Big Games was somewhat controversial.

And, as it turns out, it was also wrong. I made four mistakes, which led me to a bad conclusion, for which I apologize...two of them aren't exactly mistakes, but there are four reasons that I reached a bad conclusion. First, I did not have at that time an organized method to study this issue. I was just looking over Drysdale's record, trying to summarize it, but with no systematic approach to the issue.

Second, I did not have at that time (or for fifteen years after that) a large, organized data base by which to compare one pitcher to another. I did take the trouble to send Rob Neyer to the library and have him compile a complete game-by-game log for Drysdale's career so that I would have that to work with, and I was pretty proud of myself at the time for having invested the effort to do that. But I was studying Drysdale in isolation, as if no other pitcher existed.

Third, I focused on too few games. I focused on, as I recall, the thirteen "biggest" starts of Drysdale's career, or what I thought at that time were the thirteen biggest starts of his career...I think it was all of the games that Drysdale started from August 15 to the end of the season against a direct opponent who was in the pennant race, or something like that. It was too few games, and those games were defined by parameters, rather than by values.

Fourth, I focused on the fact that Drysdale did not "win" any of those games, meaning that he was not credited with the victory in any of them. This was just dumb, and I have no excuse for it. I got it wrong; I'm sorry.

This is the way I see the issue now. First, Drysdale started an extremely large number of Big Games. The Dodgers in that era played a huge, huge number of Big Games—a fact which I did not focus on at that time. By the standards we are using here, Drysdale made 79 Big Game starts in a relatively short career for a Hall of Famer—a higher percentage even than Andy Pettitte.

Drysdale's Big Game record, taking those 79 games as a whole, is pretty good—33 Wins, 25 Losses, 2.69 ERA. Drysdale threw 12 shutouts in Big Games, actually two more than any other pitcher.

One way I could defend myself would be to say that there were these 13 "bad big" games that I identified in 1994, but there are another 66 "sort of big" games in which he was better. But that's not true, either. Another way to study a pitcher's Big Game performance is to focus on the 35 BIGGEST games of his career. In the 35 Biggest Games of Drysdale's career (regular season), he was 17-7 with a 2.16 ERA. That's pretty good. No defense, no alibis. I was wrong, and I apologize.

5. The Ten Worst Big Game Pitchers in the Data

So, these are the guys to whom I may owe an apology the next time I write about this, if additional research undermines what I now believe:

10. **Danny Jackson**. I always liked Danny Jackson. He was a favorite of mine to watch, but...32 career starts in Big Games. 7 wins, 15 losses, 4.86 ERA.

9. **Ron Villone**. A long-term reliever, made 93 major league starts between 1999 and 2004. In Big Games he was 4-11, 5.58 ERA.

8. **Ed Whitson**. I kind of hate to pick on Ed Whitson, because he is such a media target, anyway. 45 career starts in Big Games, which is a lot, but only 8 wins, 15 losses.

7. **Armando Reynoso**, 1991-2002. Twenty starts in Big Games, 4 wins, 10 losses, 6.10 ERA.

6. **Julian Tavarez**. Red Sox fans remember him as the kind of goofy guy who would roll the ball to first base to for a 1-3 putout. The great thing about him was that he was always willing and able to take the mound. But unfortunately he had an 8.38 ERA in 10 starts in Big Games—the worst of any pitcher in the data who made ten or more starts.

5. **A. J. Burnett**. Career record of 147-132. In Big Games, 15-21, 4.61 ERA.

4. **Jerry Garvin**. Garvin, expansion pitcher in the 1970s, made only 65 starts in his career, which we could sort into the 35 biggest starts of *his* career...not 35 Big Starts, but 35 that were bigger in relative terms...and the other 30 starts. In the "other" 30 starts he was not too bad; he was 12-9. But in the "Big" 35 starts, which would be mostly the games in which he was pitching against a good team, he was 2-22 with a 5.05 ERA.

3. **Shawn Estes**. 8-10 in Big Games, but with a 5.52 ERA...the worst of any pitcher with 25 or more starts..

2. **Javier Vazquez**. Vazquez was around for a long time and always had Bert Blyleven's problem, only worse. Bert Blyleven's problem being that his won-lost record lagged far behind his strike-out/walk ratio. Overall, Vazquez had a winning record (165-160). In Big Games, he was 9-20, 5.06 ERA. This will not come as a shock to Yankee fans.

1. **Frank Tanana**. Tanana was a power-pitching phenomenon in the late 1970s who morphed into a semi-cagey veteran who stayed in the majors for 21 years, winning 240 games but losing almost as many.

In 1987, with the Tigers in a red-hot pennant race, Tanana pitched three brilliant games at the end of the year, giving up only one run in 24 innings. That was some big-time clutch pitching, but unfortunately, Tanana had also been pounded in every one of his previous eight starts, giving up 35 runs in 33 innings. His career record in Big Games: 35 starts, 5 wins, 19 losses, 4.04 ERA.

6. Some Guys Who Almost Made the Top Ten Big Game Pitchers List, but I Just Couldn't Quite Squeeze Them In

I'll run these in chart form, more or less in chronological order:

First	Last	G	IP	W	L	Pct	SO	BB	ERA	CG	ShO	Team's Record			
												W	L	R	OR
Warren	Spahn	42	320.0	28	11	.718	145	73	2.76	28	5	30	12	224	141
Ralph	Terry	31	234.3	19	7	.731	97	40	2.46	13	7	23	8	154	93
Jim	O'Toole	43	318.3	23	7	.767	205	90	3.17	12	4	29	14	234	149
Jim	Maloney	41	293.0	23	13	.639	259	112	2.30	17	8	27	14	123	115
Mike	Cuellar	38	280.0	24	9	.727	147	69	3.12	21	5	29	9	203	135
John	Candelaria	47	284.7	24	11	.686	175	69	3.32	3	1	29	18	232	172
Pascual	Perez	29	198.7	17	6	.739	146	43	2.67	6	0	19	10	130	94
Teddy	Higuera	16	116.3	12	3	.800	95	42	3.48	5	1	13	3	74	49
Bret	Saberhagen	35	252.0	20	7	.741	168	52	2.64	10	5	25	10	163	103
Dwight	Gooden	35	247.0	19	7	.731	241	71	2.66	9	5	22	13	191	116
Mike	Boddicker	27	190.3	15	7	.682	131	55	2.55	7	2	17	10	153	84
Jose	Rijo	17	117.0	11	4	.733	102	37	1.54	3	1	11	6	72	41
John	Lieber	32	210.3	22	4	.846	148	29	3.47	2	1	24	8	229	122
Derek	Lowe	52	299.0	27	13	.675	208	94	3.97	0	0	35	17	250	200
Randy	Wolf	42	254.3	22	8	.733	181	85	3.75	3	3	28	14	232	169
Chris	Carpenter	43	302.0	20	13	.606	239	67	3.22	11	5	22	21	187	179
Cliff	Lee	25	174.0	17	5	.773	123	29	2.79	3	3	19	6	135	75
CC	Sabathia	61	424.3	30	17	.638	411	124	3.29	6	1	38	23	305	210
David	Price	34	228.0	17	7	.708	198	64	2.76	3	0	25	9	168	102

And these are the records of the same pitchers in the 35 biggest games of HIS career, regardless of whether he made more or less than 35 Big Game starts:

											Team's Record			
First	Last	G	IP	W	L	Pct	SO	BB	ERA	CG	ShO	W	L	R	OR
Warren	Spahn	35	269.7	24	9	.727	123	57	2.70	24	5	26	9	188	108
Ralph	Terry	35	257.7	19	11	.633	106	52	2.72	13	7	23	12	162	118
Jim	O'Toole	35	263.3	21	4	.840	159	64	3.01	10	2	25	10	206	119
Jim	Maloney	35	252.7	19	13	.594	225	99	2.53	14	6	21	14	103	107
Mike	Cuellar	35	255.7	21	9	.700	134	66	2.99	19	5	26	9	186	122
John	Candelaria	35	216.7	17	9	.654	137	46	3.28	2	1	20	15	170	131
Pascual	Perez	35	229.3	18	10	.643	165	48	3.18	6	0	21	14	149	126
Teddy	Higuera	35	264.0	24	9	.727	223	82	2.86	14	4	26	9	153	94
Bret	Saberhagen	35	252.0	20	7	.741	168	52	2.64	10	5	25	10	163	103
Dwight	Gooden	35	247.0	19	7	.731	241	71	2.66	9	5	22	13	191	116
Mike	Boddicker	35	239.7	17	10	.630	165	70	2.85	7	2	21	14	193	117
Jose	Rijo	35	231.3	17	11	.607	184	88	2.61	4	1	17	18	134	130
John	Lieber	35	228.3	23	5	.821	162	33	3.71	2	1	26	9	240	135
Derek	Lowe	35	193.0	17	12	.586	142	63	4.48	0	0	20	15	162	148
Randy	Wolf	35	206.3	18	7	.720	154	74	3.97	2	2	23	12	186	144
Chris	Carpenter	35	243.7	16	11	.593	201	51	3.25	9	5	18	17	159	150
Cliff	Lee	35	231.3	20	8	.714	179	43	3.50	3	3	23	12	192	129
CC	Sabathia	35	245.7	16	8	.667	239	72	3.04	3	0	23	12	170	108
David	Price	35	232.0	17	8	.680	201	64	2.95	3	0	25	10	173	108

Notes about these...**Warren Spahn**, of course, we are missing a lot of data from the early part of his career; I was just surprised that his Big Game data from late in his career was so strong. **Jim O'Toole** was high on the list of pitchers who made a huge NUMBER of Big Game starts, relative to career length, 43 Big Games in 238 career starts, and here we can see that not only did he pitch a lot of Big Games, but he also won almost all of them...21 and 4 in the 35 biggest games of his career.

Jim Maloney, you should note that not only did he go 23-13 in Big Games, but that he did it while starved for run support, exactly three runs a game. Among all pitchers with 40 or more starts in Big Games, Maloney is last by far in run support. (The average is 4.56, and Luis Tiant is next-to-last at 3.68. Maloney is almost twice as far below average as any other pitcher.) Maloney posted a 2.30 ERA in Big Games, and he pitched a lot of Big Games. He was a Hall of Fame caliber pitcher; he just got hurt before his career numbers got big enough to carry him.

Pascual Perez was the pitcher I alluded to earlier who was always regarded as a head case. When Perez was murdered in the Dominican in 2012, *The New York Times* captured his image in a few paragraphs:

> *Baseball history is full of eccentrics. Jimmy Piersall once ran the bases backward to celebrate a home run. Mark Fidrych chatted with the ball as if he expected a conversation to break out. Dock Ellis pitched under the influence of LSD. Bill Lee's nickname, the Spaceman, suggested his out-thereness. And Yogi Berra became a quotable guru without even trying.*
>
> *Then there was Pascual Perez, who this week was killed, apparently in a home invasion, in the Dominican Republic. He was an odd, infectious character who demonstrated his eccentricity in good and bad ways. He hopped around the mound "as if he has a pesky mosquito in his uniform pants," Jack Curry of* The New York Times *wrote in 1991. He sprinted on and off the field. He pumped his fist after strikeouts. He pointed his finger like a gun at batters he retired. He jingled with bling. His long hair was a mass of curls. On his baseball cards, Perez looked to be having fun in a most genuine way. He was elusive. He was delightful. He was enigmatic.*
>
> *He could be a brilliant, Big Game Pitcher, but not consistently. He could throw a 95-mile-per-hour fastball and then lob a 30-m.p.h. eephus pitch.*
>
> *He will be remembered less for his occasional success on the mound than for his idiosyncrasies and, more seriously, his struggles with drugs.*

Well, they did get the Big Game pitcher in there in passing, so...good on them for doing that, and also they somehow managed to go four paragraphs before they got to the one thing that Perez was most famous for, which is the time that he got lost on the interstate surrounding Atlanta, couldn't find the ballpark and missed his scheduled start. I admire the concise description of Pascual Perez, but Perez' record in Big Games is not sporadic or patchy; it is terrific.

Teddy Higuera was injured about four years into what appeared to be a distinguished career. **Saberhagen** and **Dwight Gooden** both came up as teenagers in 1984 and won Cy Young Awards in 1985, then went on to underrated careers; I note that their Big Game records are almost identical.

Jose Rijo has the best ERA in the data of anyone with ten or more starts in Big Games (1.54 ERA). **Jon Lieber** was 22-4 in Big Games, which is obviously impressive, but that was aided by extremely strong offensive support, more than seven runs a game.

The Case for Kaat

Jim Kaat won 283 games in his major league career, won 25 games in 1966, won 20 games in 1974 and 1975, but he isn't in the Hall of Fame in large part because he wasn't perceived as a Big Game Pitcher. In fact, his record in Big Games is great. He made 53 Big Game starts in his career—more than Jack Morris—and was 27-15 in those games, 2.84 ERA. He just missed making my list of the ten best Big Game Pitchers of the last 60 years.

Let me run some of those down for you…sorry to take the time out of your day if you don't care about this, but

a) Kaat is a viable Hall of Fame candidate,
b) He deserves to have his credentials aired,
c) It is an important issue in that case, whether he was or wasn't a Big Game Pitcher, and
d) If I don't spell out the facts, people will ignore and dismiss my contention that his Big Game record is outstanding.

In 1962 the Twins were in a pennant race for the first time ever. The Twins until 1959 were the Washington Senators, and they had been among the worst teams in the American League for a quarter of a century. Kaat had made his major league debut with the Senators in 1959. In 1961 they moved to Minnesota, but still lost 91 games. In 1962, with a young team, they were in the pennant race for the first time. Here were some of Kaat's Big Games at the end of the regular season:

• August 28, 1962, the Twins are three and a half games out of first place, facing the White Sox (also in the race) in Chicago. Kaat pitches a shutout, 2-0.
• September 2, 1962 (his next start); the Twins are in second place, four games out. Kaat faces the Red Sox in Fenway Park—and beats them 5-2, complete game.
• September 7, 1962 (the next start). The Twins have closed to three games back of the Yankees. Kaat pitches another complete-game victory, beating Detroit 6-4 to keep pace with the Yankees.

•September 15, 1962. The Twins are now four games behind with 12 to play, still alive but needing to win. Kaat beats Cleveland with a complete-game six-hitter. Unfortunately, the Twins lose five of the next seven (including a loss by Kaat), and drop out of race, but Kaat's 18 wins on the season include four big wins in the closing weeks of the season.

In 1965, the Twins, after struggling for a couple of years to consolidate the breakthrough of 1962, are trying to win their first pennant in Minneapolis, the franchise's first pennant since 1933. The White Sox and Tigers are their closest pursuers. Here are some of Kaat's Big Games at the end of that regular season:

•August 26, Kaat beats the Yankees, 9-2, pitching a complete game.
•August 30, 1965, Kaat starts against the Tigers, and Twins win 3-2 in 11 innings (bullpen getting credit for the win.)
•September 3, 1965, the Twins are still in first place, the White Sox in second. The White Sox are in Minnesota to begin a crucial three-game series. Kaat starts the first game, and beats the White Sox 6-4. The White Sox win the other two games of the series, beating Mudcat Grant and Jim Perry, but Kaat's victory in the opener limits the damage.
•On September 9, 1965 (Kaat's next start...he has been held out of the last game of a series against Kansas City so he can start against the White Sox.) The Twins still in first place, the White Sox still in second. The Twins go to Comiskey. Kaat beats them again.
•September 14, 1965. Kaat wins again, beating the A's to effectively end the 1965 pennant race. The Twins win their first American League pennant, Kaat winning five straight starts in late August/early September, three of the five against the Twins closest competitors.

And here are some of his Big Games at the end of 1966:

•August 27, 1966. The Twins (67-61) are trying to hang in the race against the Orioles. Kaat pitches a 3-hit shutout against the White Sox.
•August 31, 1966; Kaat beats the Red Sox, 11-2, with another complete game victory.
•September 4, 1966. Kaat beats the Yankees, 9-2, ten strikeouts, another complete game victory. It isn't enough; the Ori-

oles continue to win almost every game, and the race is over by early September despite Kaat's 25-win season, leading the American league in starts, complete games, innings pitched and wins. But in Kaat's three biggest games of the 1966 season, he pitched three complete-game victories.

And at the end of 1967, a fantastic four-team race is shaping up among the Twins, Red Sox, White Sox and Tigers. On September 1 the Twins are a half-game behind the Red Sox, and all four teams are within a game and a half. Kaat has struggled most of the season. He enters September with 9 wins, 13 losses, 3.55 ERA. Then:

- September 1, Kaat goes all the way and beats the Tigers, 5-4, also hitting a double and scoring one of the Twins' runs. He is 10-13, 3.53 ERA.
- September 5, 1967. The Twins are now a half a game in front. Kaat beats Cleveland, another complete game, keeping the Twins a half-game ahead as the Red Sox also win. Kaat is 11-13, 3.46.
- September 9, 1967. The Twins are now tied for first with the Tigers, the Red Sox a half-game behind. Kaat beats Baltimore, 3-2, a complete game 5-hitter. He is 12-13, 3.41.
- September 13, 1967. The Twins and Red Sox are tied for first place, both teams 83-63 with 16 games left. Kaat strikes out 9 batters in 8 innings to beat the Senators, 3-2. He is 13-13, 3.37 ERA.
- September 18, 1967. Kaat pitches a ten-inning shutout against Kansas City, striking out 12 and walking no one. He is 14-13, 3.22 ERA. The Twins move into a three-way tie for first place.
- September 22, 1967. The Twins are 88-67, tied with Boston for first place with seven games to go. Kaat beats the Yankees with a complete game 7-hitter (no earned runs, two un-earned) while Boston loses, putting the Twins one game ahead with six to go. Kaat is now 15-13, 3.11.
- September 26, 1967, four days later. The Red Sox had moved back into a first-place tie with the Twins, both teams at 90-68, four games to go, with two other teams still within a game and a half of the leaders. The Twins were playing the Angels, a good team, and Kaat started for the Twins. Kaat pitched a complete-game 5-hitter, striking out 13 batters to beat the Angels, 7-3. For the third time in nine days, Kaat has put the Twins back in first place. Kaat is now 16-13, 3.07 ERA.

That was the second-biggest regular season start of Kaat's career. The biggest was the next one, September 30 at Fenway. Neither the Twins nor the Red Sox had managed to win a game in the intervening three days. The Twins were stuck at 91 wins; the Red Sox still had 90. Kaat injured his elbow and had to come out of the game in the third inning—but he was also pitching shutout baseball until he came out of the game. He ends the season at 16-13, 3.04 ERA.

The 1967 pennant race has been written about by many people—but here is what I did not know, until I took on this project. Jim Kaat in September of 1967 was as hot as Yastrzemski was. Yastrzemski in September of 1967 hit .391 with 9 homers, 24 RBI. Kaat in September of 1967 pitched 66 innings. He was 7-0, with a 1.51 ERA. He won every start except the last one, and he gave up no runs in the last one. Not too shabby.

In 1968 the Twins were never in the pennant race, and in 1969 they won the division in a walk; Kaat did not pitch any Big Games in either season, because of a late-season injury in 1969 and because the Twins didn't play many big games in either season. (The Twins, who had played 43 Big Games in 1967, played no Big Games in 1968, and only 16 in 1969.)

Kaat didn't appear in a Big Game again until September 10, 1970. The Twins were in first place in the division, Oakland in second. The Twins were playing Oakland in a double-header in Minnesota. Kaat started the second game, and beat the A's with seven strong innings (two runs). That race was over not long after that, the Twins winning it by nine games.

The Twins were not competitive in 1971. In 1972 Kaat, off to a 10-2 start, broke his hand and missed the rest of the season. When the Twins failed to compete again in 1973, they hit the re-set button and traded Kaat to the White Sox.

The White Sox were on the fringes of the pennant race. On the morning of September 4, 1973 they were 12 games out, 24 to play. By the Virtual Elimination formula they had not been eliminated. The Big Game system says it is a Big Game, which I agree is a questionable call, but...it was September, the White Sox were alive, and they were playing a divisional opponent, the Rangers. They needed a win in the worst way. Kaat pitched a 5-hit shutout.

In his next start, September 9, he faced the Twins for the first time, and he beat them. Despite this the White Sox were unable to hang in the race, and had been virtually eliminated by the time Kaat's turn came around again.

September 4, 1974, was an eerie echo of September 4, 1973. The White Sox were in exactly the same position they had been the year before—12 games behind, not Virtually Eliminated but in deep trouble. As he had the year before, Kaat pitched a shutout on that day, keeping the White Sox slim chances alive.

By September 8, 1974 (his next start), the White Sox had shaved a game off of their deficit, so the team was still alive. Kaat pitched 6 2/3 shutout innings, beating the Angels 1-0, and keeping the White Sox alive for one more day.

Kaat would pitch another shutout in his next start after that, and would very nearly pitch a shutout in the game after that and the game after that. Those were not Big Games, however, because the White Sox had been virtually eliminated by that time. Kaat would finish 1974 with 21 wins and would win 20 in 1975, but the White Sox were not competitive. He was traded to the Phillies. On September 26, 1978, by this time almost 40 years old and a spot starter, Kaat pitched six strong innings (four hits, one run) to beat the Expos. That was in the last week of the season. The Phillies held on to win the division by a game and a half over the Pirates. That was his last Big Win as a starting pitcher.

Kaat did lose some Big Games, of course, and he had another ten or fifteen wins in Big Games that I didn't tell you about. But on balance, considering all of the starts, Kaat's record in Big Games was excellent—better than Gaylord Perry's, better than Ferguson Jenkins, better than Catfish Hunter, Nolan Ryan, better than Jim Bunning or Phil Niekro or Juan Marichal, and as good as Tom Seaver. That's all I'm trying to say.

The Top Ten, Plus One

It's hard to choose…there are a lot of great pitchers with terrific records in Big Games. But these are my top ten:

11. Mike Mussina

I am, by the way, keeping silent for now on the issue of how Mike Mussina compares to Jack Morris. If Morris has a great record in Big Games, I'm not going to mention it until the end.

But Mussina certainly does. Mussina pitched in Big Games for the Orioles in 1992, 1993, 1996, 1997 and 1998, and for the Yankees every year from 2001 to the end of his career in 2008. He pitched well—3.07 ERA in 54 starts—and he won a lot more often than he lost, 27 to 13.

In Big Games, Mike Mussina defeated David Cone twice (September 2 and September 8, 2001), and Pedro Martinez twice (August 28, 2002, and September 19, 2004).

10. Bruce Kison

Bruce Kison won a Playoff Game and a World Series game for the Pirates when he was a 21-year-old rookie, 1971, and won another playoff game the next season. Those were relief appearances, but in his first four post-season appearances, Kison was 4-0 with 0.00 ERA in 20 innings. This gave Kison the reputation for being a Big Game Pitcher early in his career.

Kison was tall and thin, almost spectral, always fighting shoulder trouble, and he was never able to pitch 200 innings in a season, even once. But because of his Big Game reputation he was spotted in Big Games, and he never lost that reputation. In regular season play he was 22-7 in Big Games, 2.72 ERA.

9. Whitey Ford

It is a cliché to observe that Whitey Ford was a Big Game Pitcher, but it would be an oversight not to observe it. 36-16, 2.86 ERA.

8. Ron Guidry

We appear to be in the Yankee section of the list. Of the 35 biggest regular-season games of his career, Ron Guidry won 25. No one else in the data did. He had 39 Big Game Starts in his career, eight of them in 1978, when he was winning every start, but the other 31 in other seasons. He was 29-7 in Big Games, 3.10 ERA.

Guidry's career is like that of Gooden, Saberhagen, Valenzuela, Vida Blue; when he first appeared he was sensational, and then he kind of tapered off and was around for about ten more years, seemingly losing about 4% per season. I think those kind of pitchers are underrated by history because they create unrealistic expectations, and are compared for the rest of their careers to the pitchers they used to be.

7. Andy Pettitte

Pettitte not only pitched more Big Games than anyone else; he also performed well, with a career record of 43-18 in Big Games. Two more wins than anyone else; Clemens was 41-25.

6. Johan Santana

Johan Santana won two Cy Young Awards, was third in the voting twice, fifth once, seventh once. We can forget how good he was, and it wasn't that long ago. The Twins won their division in both of his Cy Young seasons, 2004 and 2006. They won it in 2006 by a single game, on the last day of the season. In 2008 he pitched for the Mets, when the Mets were in first place on September 19.

So Santana was pitching a lot of Big Games in those years, at a time when he was a dominant pitcher. By my count Santana has made 30 Big Game starts in his career—four with the Twins in 2003 (4-0), three with the Twins in 2004 (3-0), five with the Twins in 2005 (4-1), eight with the Twins in 2006 (which was the year the race went down to the last day of the season; 6-2), two with the Twins in 2007 (0-2), seven with the Mets in 2008 (6-1), and one with the Mets in 2010 (1-0). His teams have outscored their opponents in those games 150 to 74, and have won 24 of the 30 games. Santana's ERA in those games is 2.16, and his won-lost record is 20-4.

5. John Smoltz

The reason there are 11 pitchers in my Top Ten is that I initially overlooked Smoltz, since his regular-season Big Game record is just good, not truly outstanding. I decided it was better to wedge him in here like this and have you think I was a little slow, rather than leave him out and have you think I was stupid.

4. Don Sutton

I am as surprised as you are to see Sutton on this list, but that's why we do research. Don Sutton was born a few months after Steve Carlton, and both pitchers were National League rookies in 1966. Sutton was 324-256 in his career; Carlton, 329-244. Carlton's ERA was 3.22; Sutton's, 3.26.

In spite of those similarities, Sutton was not perceived as being comparable to Carlton. A lot of that had to do with big numbers in a season. Carlton won 20 games in a season, 27, 20, 24, 23. Carlton won four Cy Young Awards, and first-ballot selection to the Hall of Fame with 96%. Sutton would go 15-11, 16-10, 18-10; he won no Cy Young Awards and waited through five elections to get the Call.

Almost everybody, I suspect, would tell you that Steve Carlton was just more of a Big Game Pitcher than Don Sutton. OK; I'm not going to argue with you, but let me report on my research. Carlton was 6-6 in the post season; Sutton, 6-4.

In Big Games in regular season play, they made 76 starts apiece, both of them being near the all-time record for Big Game starts. Carlton was 34-32, which is somewhat misleading because his ERA was good (3.19). Sutton was 38-15, ERA of 2.66.

The two started against each other in a Big Game one time, September 5, 1980 at Dodger Stadium, both teams in the pennant race. Carlton gave up one run in 7 innings. Sutton beat him, 1-0, giving up 2 hits, no runs in eight innings, 10 strikeouts.

He started once in a Big Game against Dock Ellis, September 1, 1974, and he beat him.

He started three times in big games against Phil Niekro, and beat him twice. Sutton's teams won all three games; the third victory went to the bullpen.

He started once in a Big Game against J. R. Richard, and he beat him.

He started seven Big Games against the Big Red Machine, the Reds of the 1970s. He went 3-1 in those games, and the Dodgers won four of the seven.

Sutton never started a Big Game against Seaver or Jenkins; they were in the other division, and, at that time, teams played almost entirely inside the division the last six weeks of the season. There weren't any Big Games between the Dodgers and Reds in '75 and '76, because the Reds finished off the pennant race before there was time for any Big Games.

The record is what it is. Maybe I'm missing something, I don't know.

3. Randy Johnson

Randy Johnson had a famously poor record in Playoff Series. Although he won three games in the only World Series he ever appeared in, the wonderful World Series of 2001, he never appeared in any other World Series in part because he kept losing critical games in the playoffs. He won two games in the first round of the playoffs in 1995 against the Yankees, but then lost a game in the second round, against Cleveland. He lost two games in the first round in 1997, two more in 1998, one more in 1999. Altogether he was 7-9 in the post season, 3.50 ERA.

And that is the ONLY thing that is keeping me from naming him the greatest Big Game Pitcher of the last 60 years. If I were to say that Randy Johnson was the greatest Big Game Pitcher of my lifetime, people would say, "Well, what about all those losses in the playoffs," and they would be entirely right to say that.

But in Big Games in regular season play, Randy Johnson was the greatest pitcher ever, by far. As great as he was all the rest of the time...Big Games, he was better. He made 48 starts in Big Games. He was 30-5, 2.44 ERA, 421 strikeouts in 345 innings.

The twelve biggest regular season games that Johnson ever started, he won 11 of them. The other one, he pitched 8 innings, and left the game with a 3-3 tie.

2. Bob Gibson

I have to defend the proposition that Don Sutton was a great Big Game Pitcher; I have to defend Randy. Bob Gibson, nobody's going to argue with me.

Gibson's Big Game regular-season won-lost record isn't as good as Randy Johnson's, but it's still impressive—36-14, 2.26 ERA. Add in the dominant performances in three World Series, and he's very near the top of the list.

1. Roy Oswalt

And no, I am not just being provocative. Gibson's won-lost record in regular-season Big Games was 36-14; Oswalt's is 37-9. Gibson's teams were 40-17; Oswalt's were 46-12. Think about it: 46-12 in Big Games. Gibson's ERA was 2.26; Oswalt's was 2.63. When you adjust for context, I suspect that Oswalt wins that one. Oswalt pitched 80 fewer innings than Gibson, but struck out almost as many batters (341 to 352) and walked half as many (73 to 144).

In certain ways we are not as good at making myths now as we were a generation ago. The Wild Card system DOES create more Big Games, I believe, but sometimes it creates Big Games for second-place and third-place teams. The story lacks the clarity and symmetry of a pennant race; it is a harder story to tell.

Roy Oswalt won a tremendous number of Big Games for the Astros in the mid-2000s, but when there are six pennant races to follow and two Wild Cards, things get lost in the shuffle. Oswalt's constant drumbeat of Big Wins late in the season didn't have the impact of Bob Gibson winning 7 games in September of '64. But... just the facts. Oswalt won 80% of his Big Games. Wow.

Team Big Game Stats
Q. What is the most Big Games ever played by a team in a season?
A. 53, by the Dodgers in 1962.

Q. What is the fewest?
A. There are several teams every season which play no big games at all. Teams that are out of the pennant race by the first of August just never play Big Games, as this system defines a Big Game.

Q. Were there any such teams in 2013?
A. There were 12 of them—which is very unusual. There are always some teams that don't play any big games, but 12 is a high number.

Q. What were those teams?
A. The Astros, White Sox, Twins, Angels, and Blue Jays in the American League, and the Giants, Padres, Cubs, Brewers, Mets, Phillies and Marlins in the National League. The unusual one is the Angels, because the Angels finished 78-84, and a team that close to .500 usually gets to a few Big Games before they are wiped out. But the Angels were 16 games under .500 in mid-August, then rallied toward respectability after the race was already over.

Q. Who played the most?
A. In 2013?
Q. Yes.
A. The Cardinals. 40.

Q. What is a normal average?
A. 12, 13 per team per season.

Q. Has that changed over time?
A. It's gone up a little because of the increased number of teams and games, which just increases all of the numbers. We've gone from 16 teams to 30 and from 154 games to 162; of course that increases the number of Big Games that turn up.

Q. What is the most ever played in a league?
A. 337, by the National League in 2007. Down-to-the-wire pennant races in all three divisions. The Phillies beat the Mets by one game in the East, with Atlanta staying in the race until the third week of September. The Cubs beat the Brewers by two games in the Central, and the Diamondbacks finished just one game ahead of both the Rockies and the Giants in the NL West. The Diamondbacks and Giants thus tied for the Wild Card, necessitating a playoff before the playoffs. No team in the entire league finished 20 games behind the first-place team—whereas in 2013, five teams in each league finished more than 20 games out. And when you finish 20 games out, generally speaking, you don't play any Big Games.

Q. What other leagues had a large numbers of Big Games?

A. National League in 2001, 297. Again, close races in all three divisions.

Q. What is the highest total for a single pennant race?

A. 220, for the American League in 1967, followed by 201, for the National League in 1965. Followed by the National League in 1966, 1963, and 1964. Wonderful pennant races every season.

Q. What is the lowest total, for a league?

A. Well...the strike seasons.

Q. Other than the strike seasons?

A. The American League in 1958 had only 35 Big Games all year, all eight teams. The Yankees won by ten games, but that's misleading because the Yankees were under .500 from August first to the end of the season. The race was over by early August; the Yankees just coasted in.

Q. The numbers have gone up, over time?

A. Up and down. In the 1960s there were, in retrospect, a series of quite remarkable pennant races.

The American League in 1964 and the National League in 1965 and 1966 had terrific pennant races, but the narrative of those races is undermined by a predictable outcome. If you take the names off of the teams, the American League in 1964 had an amazing race, with three teams finishing with 99, 98 and 97 wins. But the Yankees won it, which transforms the whole thing into a yawner, whereas if the White Sox had won it, it would be a classic. The National League in 1965, even more so; the Braves finished in fifth place, at 86-76, and the Braves were in the race with two weeks to go. The Phillies finished only a half-game behind the Braves. Half the league was in the pennant race and there were a lot of odd and interesting things that happened, but the Dodgers won it, so it became just another season, just another Dodger pennant.

I was young then, and I just assumed that this was the way baseball was; there were great pennant races every year. Never thought about it. In the 1960s the average team played just over 14 Big Games per season, but this number dropped sharply in the 1970s. In retrospect, the 1969 split into divisions markedly reduced the number of Big Games, and drained the excitement out of the pennant races. What tended to happen, more years than not, was that there would be two good teams in the league, but one would be in the East and the other would be in the West, so there would be no pennant race. With two six-team divisions, you just absolutely did not get those wonderful three- and four-team pennant races that we had in the 1960s.

The 1980s were about like the 1970s, with an average of about 11 Big Games per team per season...lower because of the 1981 strike, but slightly higher if you throw out the 1981 strike.

Q. So did the Wild Card solve that problem?
A. It did. It took me a long time to understand this, and I never understood it fully until I did this study, but the Wild Card system did increase the number of Big Games per team back to about what it had been before the split into divisions in 1969. This came at a cost, because what often happens is that the best teams in the league sew up their divisions early and play few Big Games, but the second- and third-place teams continue to play Big Games until the last couple of days of the season. It might be better to have the BEST teams playing Big Games, but that's not the way it is.

But anyway, the number of Big Games per team per season is back now to a bigger number, with the Wild Card, and since the number of teams is larger, the number of Big Games is larger. By my count there have been 4,738 regular season Big Games in the last ten years, whereas in the 1970s and the 1980s there were less than 2800 per decade.

Q. Could it be *too* big?
A. It could be too big, yes. There is a "size of the human mind" problem at some point. If you have four teams focused in a single pennant race, like the American League in 1967, your mind can handle that, whereas if you have eight teams competing in three different pennant races, like the National League in 2007, you can't wrap your head around all of the details, so it loses significance. We lose the sense of these being mythic events, Yastrzemski's hot streak, Mauch starting Bunning on short rest, etc. Roy Oswalt can pitch like Bob Gibson, but he doesn't become Bob Gibson because people don't have a clear, uncluttered view of what is happening.

Q. How many Big Games did the Kansas City A's play?

A. None. By my system, the A's in their thirteen years in Kansas City never played a Big Game. Whereas the Dodgers, from 1953 through 1962, played 330 Big Games in a ten-year span.

More Analysis
(yeah, you can skip this too if you want)

I used three other ways of looking at the data, which were:

1) To use a higher standard for what constitutes a Big Game,
2) To use a lower standard for what constitutes a Big Game, and
3) To look at the 35 Biggest Games started by each pitcher, regardless of how big these games were.

Andy Pettitte started 82 Big Games; Randy Jones started only one, but Andy Pettitte still had 35 biggest games for Andy Pettitte, and Randy Jones still had 35 biggest games for Randy Jones. That way, everybody is on an even footing.

Randy Jones, in his 35 biggest games, was not good; he was 10-16, 3.65 ERA, struck out 70 batters in 240 innings and walked 54.

I love that data, for the worst reasons. I love creating "mythical seasons" or imaginary seasons, and 35 starts LOOKS like a season. A pitcher pitches well, he can win 20 games. He can strike out 200 batters, or walk 100; he can pitch 250 innings, or 300, just like a pitcher does in a season. You can create "league leaders" in every category. These are the league leaders in each category:

Innings Pitched
1. Bob Gibson, 277.2
2. Bob Lemon, 274.1
3. Mark Fidrych, 273.2

Hold on there. Mark Fidrych started only 56 games his career. His 35 "biggest" games are really just his career. Do we want to allow him in this study?

Sure we do.

4. Mel Stottlemyre, 271.2.
5. Gaylord Perry, Early Wynn and Warren Spahn, 269.2.

Wins

1. Ron Guidry, 25.
2-3-4. Warren Spahn, Teddy Higuera and Randy Johnson, 24 each.
5-6-7-8. Bob Gibson, Bob Lemon, Roy Oswalt and Jon Lieber, 23 each.

Other 20-game winners: Johan Santana, 22-5, Milt Wilcox (!), 22-9, Andy Benes, 22-6, Jim O'Toole, 21-4, Mike Cuellar, 21-9, Virgil Trucks, 21-10, Tom Sturdivant, 21-9, Whitey Ford, 21-5, Luis Tiant, 21-7, Roger Clemens, 21-7, Denny Neagle (!), 21-9, Bruce Kison, 21-5, Ian Kennedy, 21-8, Ferguson Jenkins, 20-13, Frank Lary, 20-8, Bret Saberhagen, 20-7, Earl Wilson, 20-7, Allie Reynolds, 20-9, Don Sutton, 20-7, Brandon Webb, 20-9, Cliff Lee, 20-8, Zack Greinke, 20-6, Kris Medlen, 20-5, Chien-Ming Wang, 20-7, Mark Thurmond, 20-8.

Losses

1. Chris Zachary, 23.
2-3-4. Kip Wells, Brian Matusz and Jerry Garvin, 22 each.
5. Fourteen pitchers tied with 21.

Winning Percentage

1. Randy Johnson (24-4), .857
2. Jim O'Toole (21-4), .840
3-4. Roy Oswalt and Jon Lieber (23-5), .821
5-6. Juan Guzman and Pedro Astacio (18-4), .818

Hits allowed

1. Bill Lee, 287
2. Carl Morton, 274
3-4. Jason Dickson and Sid Hudson, 273 each
5-6. Larry Sorensen and Ned Garver, 271 each.

Runs Allowed

1. Julio Santana, 154
2-3. Scott Schoeneweis and Tim Wakefield, 151 each
4-5. Mike Oquist and Bobby Jones, 150 each

Earned Runs Allowed

(Same guys, just changes the order a little)

Strikeouts
1. Randy Johnson, 306
2. Yu Darvish, 286
3. Kerry Wood, 269
4. Steve Carlton, 267
5. Nolan Ryan, 256

Walks
1. Bob Wiesler, 162 (Wiesler made only 38 major league starts, so his 35 "biggest" starts is basically just his career.)
2. Eric Plunk, 141
3. Edwin Correa, 137
4. Herb Score, 135
5. Bob Turley, 130

ERA
1. Randy Johnson, 2.01
2. Don Drysdale, 2.16
3. Mel Stottlemyre, 2.22
4. Gary Peters, 2.23
5. Joel Horlen, 2.24

Complete Games
1. Warren Spahn, 24
2. Mark Fidrych, 22
3. Connie Marrero, 21
4. Bob Lemon, 20
5. Bob Gibson, Sandy Koufax, J. R. Richard, Mike Cuellar and Walt Masterson, 19 each.

Shutouts
1-2-3-4. Bob Porterfield, Ralph Terry, Mickey Lolich and Don Drysdale, 7 each
5-6-7-8-9-10-11 J. R. Richard, Sandy Koufax, Mel Stottlemyre, Allie Reynolds, Jim Maloney, Luis Tiant and Dennis Leonard, 6 each

Wins by Team
1. Roy Oswalt, 29
2-3-4. Kris Medlen, Bill Stafford and Johan Santana, 28 each.
5-6-7-8-9-10 Ron Guidry, Randy Johnson, Whitey Ford, Mike Bielecki, Roger Clemens and Andy Benes, 27 each.

Cy Young Award

Randy Johnson

You look at the data in different ways to make sure you're not missing something by just looking at it one way. Sandy Koufax' record in all Big Games is pretty unimpressive (28-26), but in the 35 BIGGEST games of his career he was 18-8, 2.44 ERA, 250 strikeouts in 251 innings. That's much better, much more Koufaxian.

Generally, of course, you see the same things looking at the data one way that you do looking at it another. If you use a higher standard for what constitutes a "Big" game, then the leader in Big Games pitched is not Andy Pettitte but Jim Palmer (64; Pettitte has 58). If you use a lower standard, then the leader is not Pettitte or Palmer, but Steve Carlton, with 133.

That doesn't matter much; what I am looking for is changes in the way we would evaluate the Big Game Pitchers, based on their performance. I don't really see anything, other than Koufax. Using a looser standard of what is a Big Game, Roy Oswalt still has the best won-lost record (48-14), although Warren Spahn is now pushing him, at 49-15, and Dwight Gooden has entered the picture, at 41-13. I think we would evaluate almost all of the Big Game pitchers about the same, using either a higher or a lower standard for what is a Big Game, so I'm just basically going to let that data go away.

Back to Jack

OK, we have come, at last, back to the can opener which opened this particular can of worms, which is the question: Was Jack Morris, in fact, a Big Game Pitcher?

He was not.

He had the one brilliant post-season, of course, but other than that one three-week period he absolutely was not; it is not questionable, it is not debatable, it is not unclear. It does not seem likely that the conclusion could be altered by studying the question in a different way. Jack Morris did not have a great or even good record in Big Games, and the people who believe that he did believe that because they believe that, but not because there is any actual evidence for it.

In the games that our system has designated as regular season Big Games, Jack Morris made 46 starts, won 18 games, lost 19, 3.79 ERA. His teams were 24-22.

If you use a higher standard for what is a "Big Game", his record gets worse; it goes down to 10-14, although his ERA improves to 3.51. His teams won 14 of his Biggest Game Starts, lost 15. Let's look at what some of those games were.

- September 4, 1978. Tigers are 74-61, 11 games behind but still on the fringes of the pennant race with 27 games to be played. Morris, not yet established as a major league pitcher, drew the start against the Yankees at Yankee Stadium, was knocked out in the fifth inning after surrendering four runs. Tigers rallied to win the game, 5-4. Morris went back to the bullpen, and the Tigers didn't get back into a pennant race until 1982.
- September 10, 1982 Tigers, still a building team, are in a similar position, 11 and a half out with 25 to play. Morris started against Dennis Eckersley at Fenway Park and defeated the Red Sox, 6 to 4, keeping the Tigers on the fringes of the pennant race for another day or two. Tigers lost four of the next five (including one loss by Morris), and were virtually eliminated within days.
- August 28, 1983. The Tigers are truly in a pennant race for the first time in Morris' career. The Tigers are two games out of first (72-55) with 35 to play, playing the Blue Jays in Toronto; Blue Jays are in fourth place, two games behind the Tigers. Morris starts against Luis Leal. Tigers trail 2-1 going into the ninth inning, get 3 in the 9th to win the game, 4-2. Morris is 17-7, and 2-0 on this chart. Morris wins his next start, which doesn't count as a Big Game because it's out-of-division against a weak team. Next big start is September 5, 1983. Tigers are now 4 and a half games back with 26 to play. Morris starts against Cleveland. He leads 2-0 going into the 7th, gives up a run in the 7th and 2 in the 8th, loses the game 3-2; Detroit misses a chance to gain ground.
- September 9, 1983; Tigers now 5 and a half behind with 23 to play. Morris starts in Milwaukee against Moose Haas; loses the game, 2-1.
- September 13, 1983; Tigers still 5 games behind with 18 to play. Tigers at home against Cleveland. Morris starts against Rick Behenna, wins the game, 3-2, his 19th win of the season. Baltimore beats Boston twice, pulls five and a half ahead despite the Tigers' win.
- September 17, 1983; Tigers now 6 games back with 15 to play, in danger of falling out of the race. Morris starts against Dennis Eckersley in Fenway Park. Tigers lead 2-0 going into the bottom of the 7th. Morris gives up 2 in the 7th and loses the game on a Tony Armas homer in the bottom of the 8th.

- September 21, 1983; Tigers now 6 and a half back with 12 to play, tottering on the brink. Morris starts against the Orioles (Mike Boddicker) in Tiger Stadium. Morris gives up homers to Ripken and Murray in the second inning, gives up six runs in six innings, loses the game. Tigers also lose the second game of the double header, and are virtually eliminated.
- September 3, 1984; Tigers are running away with it, but the race is still sort of alive. Tigers lead the division by 8 and a half with 25 to play. Morris faces the Orioles (Storm Davis) in Tiger Stadium. Morris gives up 6 runs in 7+ innings, loses the game. The race lives another day.
- September 8, 1984; Tigers now lead by 9 and a half with 21 to play; you can argue the race is over if you want to. Morris leaves the game with an injury in the 5th inning, score tied 2-2. Tigers win it late; race is over before Morris' turn comes around again.

In 1985 and 1986 Morris did not pitch any Really Big Games. In 1985 the Blue Jays won the division at 99-62, the Tigers finishing 15 behind; they were on the fringes of the pennant race in mid- to late-August, but they were playing bad teams and out of division at the time. Morris pitched against the Blue Jays on June 30 and September 10, but June 30 is too early to be a Big Game, and by September 10 the Tigers had been virtually eliminated. And he lost both of those games, but we don't count them as Big Games.

1986, you can credit Morris with a couple of Big Wins if you want to. Morris shut out the Red Sox at Tiger Stadium on August 11, 1986; that doesn't score as a Big Game by my system, but you can certainly argue for it. The return matchup, at Fenway Park on August 16, does score as a Big Game and Morris did "win" it, although he gave up 6 runs in 7 innings.

After that Morris pitched against the Angels, Oakland, Seattle and Oakland...not only the other division, but (excepting the Angels) the worst teams in the other division. He was hit hard in all four of those games, giving up 21 runs 26.1 innings, but we don't count them as Big Games. By the time he pitched in the division again, September 11 against Milwaukee, the Tigers had been virtually eliminated.

In 1987 the Tigers were back in the race, and that race would last to the wire. Morris' first Really Big Start in 1987 was September 7, 1987, against the Orioles. The Tigers were in second place, one game out. The Orioles were non-competitive (62-74), but...September, one game out of first place; it's a Big Game. Morris pitched against Jeff Ballard, and he won that game, 12-4.

Everything from now on, 1987, is a Big Game; the race is neck and neck:

- September 12, 1987; Morris started against Bill Wegman of the Brewers. He gave up 7 runs in five and a third, lost the game.
- September 16, 1987, Morris started against Jeff Sellers of the Red Sox, pitched extremely well, and won the game, 4-1.
- September 20, 1987; the Tigers now a game and a half in front. Morris pitches against Juan Nieves of the Brewers in Tiger Stadium. Morris is hit hard; Tigers lose the game 11 to 4.
- September 24, 1987; the Tigers now a half-game behind the Blue Jays. Morris pitches against the Blue Jays in Toronto, the biggest regular-season start of his career up to this point. Morris is staked to an early 2-0 lead. In the bottom of the third he walks two, throws a wild pitch, gives up a two-run double to Rance Mulliniks, and gives up four runs, loses the game 4-3.
- September 28, 1987. By now the Tigers are two and a half behind with 7 games to play. Morris pitches against the Orioles (a bad team) and John Habyan (not a great pitcher) at Tiger Stadium. He loses the game 3-0, not exactly his fault, but... he walked five, Big Game, and he lost.

In the tightest pennant race of his career, Morris has now lost three straight starts and four out of five. In spite of Morris, though, the Tigers hold on, as Doyle Alexander and Walt Terrell are both winning every start. On the day that Morris loses to Baltimore the Blue Jays also lose, so the Tigers stay two and a half behind, six to play. The next day Frank Tanana beats Baltimore, and the Tigers pull to within a game and a half, five to play. Both teams lose on September 30 (Wednesday); the race holds its position with four to play. On Thursday Terrell beats the Orioles, the Blue Jays are idle, and the Tigers close the gap to one game.

The schedule makers have got it right this time; Toronto will play three games in Detroit to close the season. Friday, October 2, Doyle Alexander, obtained from Atlanta for a minor league pitching prospect, beats Jim Clancy, 4-3, and the race is tied. Saturday, Morris starts against Mike Flanagan. The game is tied, 2-2 through 9 innings. Morris leaves at that point. Flanagan pitches the 10th, the 11th; game still tied 2-2. Alan Trammell wins the game with a bases-loaded single in the bottom of the 12th. MVP voters fail to notice. Tigers are a game ahead with one to play. Tanana pitches a shutout in the last game of the season, and the Tigers win the division.

They won the division, but it's at least as much despite what Jack Morris did in Big Games as because of it. For the Tigers in September/October, 1987:

- Matt Nokes hit .308 with 7 homers,
- Darrell Evans hit 9 homers and drove in 25 runs,
- Alan Trammell hit .417 (53/127) with 7 homers and 20 RBI,
- Doyle Alexander went 6-0 with a 1.09 ERA,
- Walt Terrell also went 6-0, albeit with a 3.58 ERA,
- Lou Whitaker, Kirk Gibson and Tom Brookens also played well, and even Frank Tanana turned in three brilliant games at the end of the month,
- Jack Morris was 3-4 with a 3.09 ERA.

In 1988 the American League East had one of its greatest pennant races, with five teams in it all the way. Morris struggled through the first half of the season, with a 5.33 ERA through July 19, then had a long string of starts against the other division. He made eleven starts in July and August, 1988, nine of them against the American League West. He did pitch very well in beating the Red Sox on August 5; we don't mark that as a Big Game, but you can if you want to. But if you mark that one as a Big Game, you certainly have to mark his next start against the division, which was against the Brewers on August 27, and he lost that one, or anyway the Tigers lost it.

Morris' first game in 1988 that meets our standard of a Big Game was against the Blue Jays at Tiger Stadium, September 5. The Tigers and Red Sox were now tied for first place, both teams at 75-61. Morris faced off against Mike Flanagan of the Blue Jays. He gave up 11 hits, 4 runs in eight innings; the Tigers lost in extra innings.

By the time he started again, September 10, the Tigers were two and a half behind; still a Big Game, obviously. Morris started against the Yankees at Yankee Stadium. The Tigers staked him to a 4-2 lead. He gave up 11 hits and 7 runs in six and a third, lost the game 9-4.

On September 16, Morris started against the Orioles at Tiger Stadium. The Orioles are still a bad team; they're on their way to 100 losses. He was knocked out of the game in the third inning, after surrendering a three-run homer to Eddie Murray. The Tigers, down 5-1 at the time Morris left the game, rallied to win.

He started against the Indians on September 20; the Indians are the other non-competitive team in the division. By now the Tigers are six games behind with 12 to play; they are on the border of being eliminated. He beats the Indians, 3-1.

His next start is against the Orioles on September 25. The Tigers are five back with eight to play; they're really out of it, but we err on the side of caution and pretend they are not. Morris beats the Orioles 2-1, and we give him credit for a Big Win, because there is one week left in the season and the Tigers have not been officially eliminated. The race is over before Morris starts again, so...that's it for 1988.

In 1989 the Tigers lost 103 games; Morris was 6-14. Morris didn't start another Big Game until September 12, 1990, against the Orioles, and that, again, is a game that we wince to describe as a Big One. The Tigers were ten and a half out with 19 to play. We err on the side of caution; we say that the Tigers are NOT virtually eliminated, although if they are not they are awfully close to it, but if they're in the race in mid-September, it's a Big Game. In any case he lost, dropping his record on the season to 11-18, and the Tigers were certainly out of the race then. Morris won his last four starts, against four teams that were also just playing out the string, and finished the season 15-18.

I was writing annual baseball books then, a few of you will remember, and I went out of my way that winter to defend Jack Morris against the many people who were saying that his career was finished. "He's not finished," I wrote, "He can still win 18 games if he lands with a competitive team." Not sure the phrasing was exact; something very close to that. He did in fact sign with a competitive team, after I wrote that, and then he did in fact win 18 games. Blind pig; acorn.

In 1991 Morris pitched for the Minnesota Twins, who won the American League West in a fairly easy contest, winning by nine games. The Twins went on to win the World Series, Jack Morris being the World Series MVP after pitching a ten-inning shutout in the 7th Game of the World Series, perhaps the greatest Game 7 performance in World Series history.

It was that post-season, of course, that established Morris in the minds of sports writers as a Big Game Pitcher—two wins in the playoffs, two more in the World Series, including the Game 7 masterpiece.

But as to the regular season contests...well, it is kind of the same stuff we have been seeing. After making three straight starts against the worst teams in the other division (August 27, September 1 and September 7), Morris made his first Big Game start of 1991 against the Rangers on September 12. The Rangers were over .500 and in the Twins' division, although the race was not really close.

The 44-year-old Nolan Ryan started for the Rangers. Morris gave up a three-run homer in the first inning, lost the game 4-3. September 17, 1991 Morris started against the Royals (Bret Saberhagen). Saberhagen beat him, 4-1. September 22, 1991. The Twins are ahead by seven games with 13 to play, but since we err on the side of caution, we're going to say that the race is not over. Morris beats the Rangers, 8 to 4. We are crediting him with a Big Win.

That winter Morris was a free agent again. After two poor years in Detroit, 1989-1990, Morris was just looking for whatever he could get. He signed a one-year contract with the Twins, who had finished last in 1990, for a reported $3 million, which in baseball we refer to as a measly $3 million, because we have lost our marbles. The Twins—and Morris—had caught lighting in a coffee pot. Morris was good, and the Twins leaped from last to first to World Series champions, and Morris was a free agent again. He signed a two-year-contract with Toronto for just short of $10 million.

Toronto was the defending champion in the American League East. They needed a Big Game Pitcher to carry them all the way, and Morris was their Big Game Pitcher.

Morris made his first Big Game start for the Blue Jays on August 11, 1992, against the Orioles. The Orioles were back in contention. Camden Yards was open (although this game was played at the Skydome); the Orioles were back in business. The Blue Jays were in first place, 66-46; the Orioles were in second, three games back. Morris started for the Blue Jays against Alan Mills, gave up three runs in the fourth inning, and lost the game.

The Blue Jays played Cleveland next—a non-competitive team, and it's August, so that isn't a Big Game—then played a series against the Brewers, the other good team in their division; the three good teams in the AL East in 1992 were the Blue Jays, the Orioles and the Brewers. Morris beat the Brewers with 7 strong innings (August 22, 1992), putting the Blue Jays three games ahead of the pack.

During this time, the Blue Jays played several series against the other division...the White Sox, the Twins, the Royals, the Rangers. They got back inside the division in mid-September. September 17, 1992, the Blue Jays were three games ahead with 15 to play. Morris started against the Cleveland Indians. The Blue Jays gave him 4 runs in the first inning. Morris gradually squandered the lead. After 9 innings it was 5-5. Morris left the game. The Blue Jays won it in the 10th. The next three games:

- September 23, 1992. The Blue Jays are now four ahead of the Brewers, five and a half ahead of the Orioles. Morris started against the Orioles at Camden Yard. He gave up a bases-loaded double in the third inning, lost the game 4-1.
- September 27, 1992; the Blue Jays are up two and a half with five games to play. Morris started against the Yankees at Yankee Stadium, and beat them 12 to 2.
- October 2, 1992; the Blue Jays are two games ahead with three to play. Morris started against the Tigers (75-84) in Toronto. The Blue Jays score six runs in the first two innings to take a 6-0 lead. Morris gives up 6 runs in 6 innings, turning the game into a nail-biter, but is credited with the victory in an 8-7 game that clinches the division. Morris finishes the season 21-6.

Morris did not pitch well in the 1992 post-season, posting a 6.57 ERA in the playoffs, 8.44 in the World Series, and failing to win any of his four post-season starts. The Blue Jays, however, win all four World Series games that Morris *doesn't* start, and win the World Series. Morris' conspicuous failures in Big Games (in 1992) are overlooked and forgotten; he's a World Series winner for the second straight season.

Morris' career collapsed in 1993 (7-12, 6.19) ERA, and he never started another Big Game, although two of his starts in August of 1993 are line calls for Big Game status (Morris was raked over the coals in both outings, if you insist on knowing.)

Bert Blyelven...well, Blyleven's record in Big Games isn't great, either. It's better than Morris's, but it's still not great. Blyleven in Big Games was 20-18, 3.08 ERA. He had the same problem in Big Games that he had in other games: you need runs to win. Blyleven is in the bottom 20% of pitchers in terms of run support average in Big Games. He still managed to win more of them than he lost.

Jack Morris became famous as a Big Game Pitcher based on

a) four good starts in the 1991 post-season, and
b) the fact that the people who wanted to put him in the Hall of Fame had to have something they could say, so they claimed that he was a Big Game Pitcher.

But other than those four starts in the 1991 post-season, there is nothing there. His record in Big Games, other than the 1991 post-season, isn't good; it is actually very poor. Yes, he did win *some* Big Games; every pitcher who has a real career does, even Frank Tanana. Jon Lester has won far more Big Games in his career than Jack Morris did, in a career that isn't yet half as long. Doyle Alexander was 0-5 in the post season—but he still won more Big Games than Morris did.

If you want to advocate for a pitcher being in the Hall of Fame based on his performance in Big Games, advocate for Ron Guidry, or Jim Kaat, or Mickey Lolich, or Mike Mussina.

———

GOING OUT ON TOP

by Bill James

———•———

Mariano Rivera retired after the 2013 season despite saving 44 games with a 2.11 ERA—the best "last season" ever for a relief pitcher, regardless of age, although Robb Nen was almost as good. Anyway, a few years ago I chose an All-Star team of players based on how they played in their last season in the majors, so I'll add The Sandman to the team. Also, I'd like to announce publicly that if Miguel Cabrera would retire now, I would guarantee him a spot on the team. Just sayin'...an All-Star team of players who retired, were banned or died after having played well and played almost full time in their last season, based only on their performance in that last season.

Catcher—Dave Nilsson, last year 1999, 21 homers, 62 RBI, .309. .954 OPS. Reason for retirement: Had serious injury, went back to Australia, got real fat and wasn't able to get back in the game.
Alternate—Darren Daulton, last year, 1997, 14 homers, 63 RBI, .263. Reason for retirement: Bad knees, colorful lifestyle.
Alternate—Thurman Munson, last year,1979, 3 homers, 39 RBI, .288. Reason for retirement: Poor aviation skills.

First Base—Will Clark, 2000, .319, 21 homers, 70 RBI. Reason for retirement: I think he just didn't want to become a steroid junkie in order to stay in the game.
Alternate—Hank Greenberg, 1947, .249, 25 homers, 74 RBI, 104 walks. Reason for retirement: High personal standards.
Alternate—Roy Cullenbine, 1947, .224, 24 homers, 24 homers, 78 RBI. Reason for retirement: Managers in that era genuinely

77

didn't understand that his 137 walks/.401 on base percentage made him a valuable man despite his low batting average.

Alternate—Tony Horton, 1970, .269, 17 homers, 59 RBI. Reason for retirement: Serious mental health issues; institutionalized.

Alternate—George Brett, 1993, .266, 19 homers, 75 RBI. Reason for retirement: Age, high personal standards.

Second Base—Bobby Doerr, 1951, 13 homers, 73 RBI, .289. Reason for retirement: Dignity, injuries.

Alternate—Ray Durham, 2008, 6 homers, 45 RBI, .299. Reason for retirement: Not sure; I remember there was a big surplus of second basemen in the market that winter, and I think his agent may have missed the opportunity to land a good spot.

Alternate—Joe Gedeon, 1920, 0 homers, 61 RBI, .292. Reason for retirement: Black Sox Scandal.

Alternate—Joey Cora, 1998, 6 homers, 32 RBI, .276, 111 runs scored. Reason for retirement: Not sure.

Third Base—Buck Weaver, 1920, 2 homers, 74 RBI, .331, 208 hits. Reason for retirement: Black Sox Scandal.

Alternate—Tony Boeckel, 1923, 7 homers, 79 RBI, .298. Reason for retirement: Killed in a car wreck.

Alternate—Doug Rader, 1977, 18 homers, 67 RBI, .251. Reason for retirement: Don't know.

Shortstop—Ray Chapman, 1920, 3 homers, 49 RBI, .303 average. Reason for retirement: Killed by a pitch.

Alternate—Sam Wise, 1893, .311, 5 homers, 77 RBI, .311, 102 runs scored. Reason for retirement: Don't know.

Left Field—Joe Jackson, 1920, .382, 12 homers, 121 RBI. Reason for retirement: Black Sox scandal.

Alternate—Ted Williams, 1960, .316, 29 homers, 72 RBI. Reason for retirement: Age.

Alternate—Barry Bonds, 2007, .276, 28 homers, 66 RBI, 132 walks. Reason for retirement: Huge jackass, nobody wanted him around if he wasn't going to hit .350 with 40 homers.

Alternate—Indian Bob Johnson, 1945, 12 homers, 74 RBI, .280. Reason for retirement: End of World War II brought the players back from Europe and created unusual pressures for roster space.

Center Field—Kirby Puckett, 1995, .314, 23 homers, 99 RBI, .314. Reason for retirement: Loss of vision in right eye due to central retinal vein occlusion.

Alternate—Lyman Bostock, 1978, .296, 5 homers, 71 RBI. Reason for retirement: Murdered.

Alternate—Happy Felsch, 1920, .338, 14 homers, 115 RBI, 40 doubles, 15 triples. Reason for retirement: Scandal.

Right Field—Jermaine Dye, 2009, 27 homers, 81 RBI, .250. Reason for retirement: Why Dye no job?

Alternate—Larry Walker, 2005, .289, 15 homers, 52 RBI. Reason for retirement: Aging, bad knees, had made a lot of money.

Alternate—Buzz Arlett, 1931, .313, 18 homers, 72 RBI. Reason for retirement: Returned to minors; was probably making more money as a superstar in the minors than playing for the Phillies.

Alternate—Roberto Clemente, 1972, .312, 10 homers, 60 RBI. Reason for retirement: Killed in plane crash.

Alternate—Paul O'Neill, 2001. 21 homers, 70 RBI, .267. Reason for retirement: Age, dignity.

DH—Albert Belle, 2000, .281, 23 homers, 103 RBI. Reason for retirement: Injury. Belle had a big-bucks contract which was insured so that his team was paid by the insurer if Belle couldn't play at all. If Belle had tried to come back and had played at a diminished level, as 99% of injured players do, that would have let the insurance company off the hook, thus costing his team millions of dollars.

Starting Pitcher—Sandy Koufax, 1966, 27-9, 1.73 ERA, 317 strikeouts. Reason for retirement: Arthritis, chronic fluid buildup in the elbow.

Starting Pitcher—Eddie Cicotte, 1920, 21-10, 3.27 ERA. Reason for retirement: Black Sox scandal.

Starting Pitcher—Mike Mussina, 2008, 20-9, 3.37 ERA. Reason for retirement: Too old to Rock and Roll.

Starting Pitcher—Lefty Williams, 1920, 22-14, 3.91 ERA. Reason for retirement: Black Sox scandal.

Fifth Starter—Larry French, 1942, 15-4, 1.82 ERA. Reason for retirement: World War II. I think French actually was an Intelligence Officer in World War II, and stayed in the Navy after the War, eventually retired as a Navy Captain.

Starting Pitcher—Henry (About) Schmidt, 1902, 22-13, 3.83 ERA. Reason for retirement: Texan who hated the East, didn't want to come East to play baseball any more.

Closer—Mariano Rivera, 2013, 6-2, 44 Saves, 2.11 ERA. Reason for retirement: No mountains left.

Closer—Robb Nen, 2002, 6-2, 43 Saves, 2.20 ERA. Reason for retirement: Injury.

Closer—Steve Olin, 1992, 8-5, 29 Saves, 2.34 ERA. Reason for retirement: Killed in a boating accident.

As you can see, for a productive player to retire has been much, much more common in the last fifteen years than it was before 1995. Part of this may be that some players did not want to continue taking steroids in order to stay in the game. Another part may have been that the very high salaries of modern baseball make it unnecessary for an aging player to hang on after his best days are behind him.

Others of note: Dave Orr, 1890, Ed Konetchy, 1921, Sam Dungan, 1901, Joe Adcock, 1966, Del Pratt, 1924, Scott Brosius, 2001, Al Rosen, 1956, Joe Wood, 1922, Curt Walker, 1930, Ty Cobb, 1928, Steve Evans, 1915, Bill Lange, 1899, Bill Joyce, 1898, Perry Werden, 1897, Piggy Ward, 1894, Ecky Stearns, 1889, Charlie Ferguson, 1887, Joe DiMaggio, 1951, Mickey Mantle, 1968, Chili Davis, 1999, Johnny Dickshot, 1945, Eddie Morgan, 1934, Bill Keister, 1903, Irv Waldren, 1901, Reggie Smith, 1982, Bernie Williams, 2006, Johnny Hodapp, 1933, Ross Youngs, 1926. Pitchers: Jim Hughes, 1902, Britt Burns, 1985, Allie Reynolds, 1954, John Tudor, 1990, Paul Derringer, 1945, Larry Jackson, 1968, Ed Doheny, 1903, Vin Lingle Mungo, 1945, Phil Douglas, 1922, Jeff Zimmerman, 2001, J. R. Richard, 1980, Spud Chandler, 1947.

———·——

LET ME OFFEND YOU

by Bill James

———·———

Am I the only one who ever notices this...if you want cheddar cheese that has a good, strong flavor, you have to buy the one marked "mild". For some reason...not just one brand...if you buy the cheddar cheese marked "sharp" or "extra sharp", it is almost tasteless, whereas if you buy the cheese that is marked "mild", it has a much stronger taste. I've never been able to figure that out, and I keep buying the "sharp" cheddar, because I like a stronger taste and keep expecting the world to make sense, but then it never does. Doesn't anybody else ever notice this?

As you get older, one of the things that happens to you is that all kinds of things that seem annoying or offensive become commonplace, apparently because younger people aren't sufficiently offended by them, while all kinds of things that *don't* seem to me to be at all offensive are suddenly labeled as offensive and written outside the rules, for reasons that frankly mystify us old folk.

I'm not talking about vulgarity on TV or anything; heck, I'm used to that. I'm talking about going to the grocery store, and being expected to scan your own groceries and check yourself out. Am I the only one who doesn't *want* to scan my own groceries? Am I the only one who feels like I am certain to screw something up and be arrested on the way out of the store for not paying for my Lucky Charms and cheddar cheese?

I guess it's the modern world; nothing I can do about it.

On the "stuff that has inexplicably become intolerable" side, I read about some poor woman in Connecticut who had a job reviewing college-application essays and was fired for mocking some of the essays on Facebook. Somebody wrote in a college-application essay about going camping and having to overcome his fear of urinating in the outdoors, and she was making fun of him for choosing to write about this in a college admissions essay.

Well...what's wrong with that? I mean, it's not like she mentioned his name or made fun of him in person or anything. Isn't this more rationally regarded as a contribution toward educating kids about the process? My point is that by firing her for discussing this in public, the university is inhibiting the free flow of information which is potentially valuable to kids who are trying to figure out how to write a college admissions essay. If you're writing a college admissions essay and you are considering whether you should write about learning to urinate outdoors, isn't it better that you *know* that this is an asinine idea and that the woman who reviews the essay is going to throw your application in the trash barrel and make fun of you, rather than being allowed to imagine that whatever the hell comes into your head is an OK thing to write about? I mean, society tolerates that kind of thing, the next thing you know you'll have professional writers writing about buying cheddar cheese.

The one that really gets me, though, is this "scandal" about college basketball coaches pushing or slapping one of their players in the chest. You're kidding, right? Do basketball players break that easily these days?

I'm not saying that in my day the coaches would kick you in the butt or anything, although, now that you mention it, in my day the coaches would kick you in the butt just to get your attention. But how can a level of contact that is one-fortieth the force which is commonplace *in* the game be considered horribly offensive if it occurs on the sidelines of the game, between friends? It doesn't seem to make any sense.

Football coaches are fired for screaming at their players? Really? Why? I mean...the players get IN the game and beat hell out of each other. Why is it offensive, all of a sudden, if a football coach grabs one of his charges by the front of the shirt and tells him to pull his head out of his ass? I know I'm old and irrelevant, but...I don't get it.

———·———

Hot Hand Streaks

by Bill James

———

Here's a question I got in the "Hey, Bill" section of Bill James Online:

> *"Since hitting a baseball requires such coordination of many moving body parts, and it is easy for a piece (and therefore the whole mechanism) to get out of whack, do you think the clusters of hits we take to be hot streaks are just the player executing at a maximum level?"*

That's actually a good argument in the way it is stated, and there is a kernel of truth in it. I relate this to a sport which is more at my athletic level, which is pool. I have a pool table in my basement, and I run the table several times a day, and count how many shots it takes me to knock down 15 balls. Sometimes, once in a while, it is 15 shots—I have done it in as few as 11—and sometimes it takes 40 shots. Or even more.

I am 100% certain that not ALL of this variance is random. I am 100% certain that I fall into unproductive habits, as I am playing, that make me less effective—three of them specifically. I start "sawing" the stroke, pushing the back end of the cue down instead of sending it straight forward into the cue ball. I start "jerking" the shots, rather than shooting smoothly. There are some shots for which it is the best approach to flick the cue quickly forward and then jerk it quickly back, but that's about 15% of the shots, and I find myself doing it repeatedly when it is not appropriate. Third, I start rushing from shot to shot without taking the time to think through, before each shot, how I want to approach the shot, how I want to spin the ball, where I want to leave the cue ball to set up the following shot, etc. I know that I do these three things (and have some lesser included offenses); I have known it for years, but I still fall into these bad habits, and find myself missing shots.

Shouldn't I believe, then, that baseball players fall into similar bad habits from swing to swing, and that this makes them less effective sometimes than at other times?

Yes, I should believe that, and I do believe it. I also believe, for what it is worth, that a batter's level of effectiveness can vary, to an extent, because of "petty confidence," petty confidence being the transient, unreliable type of confidence that may be here today and totally gone by Sunday. I don't question but that these are real variables, and also, players are often playing with manageable injuries that don't prevent them from competing but may prevent them from performing at the level at which they might otherwise reach. I don't doubt that there are additional performance variables that I have not mentioned, but which some master of the obvious will find it necessary to point out to me.

At the same time, there is also the tendency of hits (and all other performance elements) to form random clusters, so then the performance variation has both real and artificial elements. The question is, to what extent, in watching the games, are we seeing what is real, and to what extent are we seeing an illusion created by random clusters?

Suppose that you take a player's statistics and re-organize his at bats at random...or suppose that you take his Start-a-Madic, ASPC or Ethan Allen's magic spinning wheel game card and recreate a thousand at bats for him. You will find, absolutely and without question, that there is just as much up and down variation in the random performance as in the player's actual record. This has been studied hundreds of times. There is a very good web site devoted to the issue, the Hot Hand Web Site (http://thehothand.blogspot.com, maintained by Texas Tech professor Alan Reifman). I don't want to overstate the study; the Hot Hand phenomenon has been studied hundreds of times by dozens of different researchers, and occasionally one of us thinks we possibly have found some tiny and elusive difference between the "actual" and simulated data. But for the most part, those studies always show that the variance in the real-life performance is identical to the variance that would be expected if nothing was operating except the normal randomization.

This is not an absolutely convincing argument that nothing is going on here except random variation. It is certainly possible for other effects to mimic the patterns of random variation closely enough that it might be difficult to distinguish between the two, and it is certainly more than possible that might be difficult to distinguish between pure random variation and some mix of random and causal variation. But the question becomes, then, how much causal variation is it reasonable to think might be completely hidden in a mix of causal and random variation?

Well, if it was 50-50, it would be extremely easy for us to distinguish between the patterns in the two sets of data. We know how much random variation can be found in any data set; that's a pretty basic and easy thing to calculate or at least estimate. If you add a second level of variation equal to the first, it will create obviously non-random patterns.

If it 70-30—in other words, if the causal variation was roughly half the size of the random variation—that, again, would be easy to distinguish from pure random variation. Even if it was 90-10, we should be able to distinguish between that and pure random variation. If it was 99-1, maybe we would have a hard time telling one from the other.

So when you see the variations in performance, what is it that you are seeing? You're seeing randomness...not pure and absolute randomness, perhaps, but largely randomness. 95% or 99% of what you are seeing is just random variations in performance.

There is another way to approach the issue. How much variation in batting performance is it reasonable to think might occur due to things like petty confidence and a hitter falling into bad habits?

Well, I don't know, exactly, but .270 hitters have months in which they hit .400. Marquis Grissom in June of 1994 hit .385 (47 for 122). Johnny Damon in 2000 hit almost .500 for a solid month. It is not reasonable to think that players actually reach that level of performance ability. If a player could become a .400 hitter for a month, somebody would hit .400 every month. Somebody would hit .400 in his career.

Johnny Damon was essentially the same hitter in 2011 that he was in 1996, and every year in between. It is not reasonable to think to that he suddenly, for a few weeks in his career, became something radically and totally different and then somehow, time after time, returned to exactly what he always had been. He is not a shape shifter. It is much more reasonable to believe that he was the same player or essentially the same player throughout but that he simply had a cluster of superlative games that made him look different for a short period of time.

We know that the standard deviation of batting average in a season, for players who bat 500 or more times, is 27 points. It is not reasonable to suppose that hitters go from being 3 standard deviations above the norm in one month to 3 standard deviations below the norm the next month. It is even less reasonable to suppose that a hitter flips from standard deviations above to standard deviations below from week to week (in terms of his true underlying ability), but somehow finds himself more or less in the same position time after time, given 600 plate appearances.

Let's go back to the issue of the variation that occurs in my pool playing from game to game, which might be analogous to the variation that occurs in your golf game if you are one of them golfer types. How long does it take you to fix a glitch in your putting style, given that you have a certain level of ability as a putter? I do fall into bad habits as a pool player, and this does cost me a few shots now and then, but I also spot these problems and fix them on a pretty short schedule. 30, 40 shots; I'm going to figure out what I am doing wrong, and get it right.

If we assume that major league hitters spot the flaws in their swings and fix them on a similar schedule in terms of the number of swings, what is that going to take? A couple of games, maybe?

Look, Yasiel Puig

a) is not a .400 hitter, and
b) is not temporarily a .400 hitter, either.

He's a .280 hitter, probably, maybe a little less. He doesn't temporarily become something other than what he is just because a string of ground balls scoot through the infield and a bunch of Dodger fans are not strong enough to blow away the smoke. I don't actually become a good enough pool player to run the table in 15 shots; it's just something that happens once in a while. Hot streaks and slumps are smoke and mirrors. It's not that there is nothing there; it is more like random variance is New York City and the actual up and down changes in ability are Immokalee, Florida. When you talk about the people who live in New York City and Immokalee, you're mostly talking about the Big Apple.

(Post-season note, 2013.) I may have underestimated the great Yasiel Puig.

THE ANALOGY OF THE FISHERMAN

by Bill James

———·—·———

There was a man who loved to fish, and one day he was so fortunate as to find an absolutely wonderful fishing hole. Some months later he was telling his friend about it. "It has everything you could possibly want in a fishing spot," he said. "It is cool and shaded. There is never anyone there. It has lots of food for the fish to eat and underground shelter in which fish can live and breed. There is a brook that feeds into a deep pool at one end. It's just perfect."

"Do you catch a lot of fish there?" asked his friend.

"Oh, no," replied the fisherman. "I've never actually caught a fish there. But I keep going back, because I've never seen such a perfect spot for fish to live in."

Look, it is easy to explain why Ground Ball pitchers *should* be effective pitchers.

The problem is, there are no fish there.

Allow me to rant for a few minutes here without any evidence. We'll get to the evidence later; I'm just trying to frame the debate. Any analyst can give you a long list of reasons why ground ball pitchers should be the best pitchers. The problem is, they're not.

Make a list of the best pitchers in baseball. Make a list of the best pitchers in baseball, in any era, and what you will find is that 80% of them are *not* ground ball pitchers. They're fly ball pitchers. Tom Seaver was not a ground ball pitcher. Bob Gibson was not a ground ball pitcher. Randy Johnson was not a ground ball pitcher. Justin Verlander is not a ground ball pitcher. Pedro Martinez was not a ground ball pitcher. Roger Clemens was not a ground ball pitcher. David Cone was not a ground ball pitcher. Dwight Gooden was not a ground ball pitcher. Catfish Hunter was not a ground ball pitcher. Steve Carlton was not a ground ball pitcher.

Greg Maddux, of course, was a ground ball pitcher, and there have been a few others, like Kevin Brown. The vast majority of good pitchers are not ground ball pitchers, and the vast majority of ground ball pitchers are not good pitchers.

What I have never understood about ground ball pitchers, and do not understand now, is why they always get hurt. Show me an *extreme* ground ball pitcher, a guy with a terrific ground ball rate, and I'll show you a guy who is going to be good for two years and then get hurt. I'm not saying this about Chien-Ming Wang and Brandon Webb now; I was saying this *before* Chien-Ming Wang and Brandon Webb. They're just the latest examples. Mark Fidrych. Randy Jones. Ross Grimsley. Mike Caldwell. Rick Langford. Lary Sorensen. Clyde Wright. Fritz Peterson. Dave Roberts. They're great for two years, and then they blow up. Always.

Always? Well...Tommy John. If your defense argument here is a guy who is famous for having a surgery named after him, I'm not sure I'm convinced. Maddux and Glavine, sure, but Maddux was not an extreme ground ball pitcher until the last two or three years of his career. I don't know whether Glavine was or not.

Derek Lowe? Derek Lowe was sensational in 2002; the rest of his career he's a .500 pitcher. You take Derek Lowe; I'll take Verlander.

Look, I'm not really saying that there aren't *any* good ground ball pitchers. What I am saying is that being a ground ball pitcher is not an advantage. It's a disadvantage.

The 2012 Cleveland Indians loaded up on ground ball pitchers. How'd that work out? They finished 68-94 with a 4.79 ERA.

I posted a rant like this in August, 2010, to which Tom Tango replied "does this mean that you would expect Adam Wainwright to not age as gracefully as other great pitchers?" Months later, Adam Wainwright had Tommy John surgery. He returned in 2012 and was outstanding again in 2013.

Let's go look at the evidence.

The Evidence

OK, it turns out that I am more wrong than right. I have this prejudice against ground ball pitchers, which I have had for a long time and I have written about before. It occurred to me that I should do a study to see whether the facts match up with my belief system.

My belief, simply stated, is that

1) All things considered, you are better off avoiding ground ball pitchers, and
2) Ground ball pitchers on the whole tend to be less successful than non-ground ball pitchers.

How do we test these propositions?

Here's what I did. I formed two groups of pitchers, without any regard to their ground ball rates. The two groups of pitchers were

a) The 50 best pitchers in major league baseball in the years 2002 to 2011, which we will call the Gold Group, and
b) The 25 pitchers from the same years who best exemplified the idea of staying around in the majors, pitching a lot of innings without ever doing very much, who we will call the Blue Group.

My theory is that Blue Group will be significantly more dependent on ground balls than is the Gold Group.

How I formed the groups is not a critical issue; I am counting on it being self-evident that these are highly successful pitchers. First, these are the 50 pitchers that I identified as being the most successful pitchers in the major leagues in the years 2002 through 2011:

Josh Beckett	Trevor Hoffman
Mark Buehrle	Tim Hudson
Matt Cain	Jason Isringhausen
Chris Carpenter	Josh Johnson
Roger Clemens	Randy Johnson
Bartolo Colon	Clayton Kershaw
Francisco Cordero	John Lackey
Eric Gagne	Cliff Lee
Roy Halladay	
Cole Hamels	Jon Lester
	Ted Lilly
Dan Haren	Tim Lincecum
Felix Hernandez	Derek Lowe

Greg Maddux	Curt Schilling
Pedro Martinez	Jason Schmidt
Jamie Moyer	John Smoltz
Mike Mussina	
Joe Nathan	Joakim Soria
Roy Oswalt	Jose Valverde
	Javier Vazquez
Jonathon Papelbon	Justin Verlander
Jake Peavy	Billy Wagner
Andy Pettitte	Adam Wainwright
Mariano Rivera	Jered Weaver
Francisco Rodriguez	Brandon Webb
CC Sabathia	Randy Wolf
Johan Santana	Carlos Zambrano

The Blue Group—pitchers who were around a long time but never really did a whole lot—consisted of:

Jeremy Affeldt	Rodrigo Lopez
Miguel Batista	Jason Marquis
Jeremy Bonderman	
Jose Contreras	Gil Meche
Aaron Cook	Guillermo Mota
	Oliver Perez
Doug Davis	Nate Robertson
Kyle Farnsworth	Carlos Silva
Josh Fogg	
Ryan Franklin	Jeff Suppan
LaTroy Hawkins	Bret Tomko
	David Weathers
Mark Hendrickson	Jeff Weaver
Scott Linebrink	Jamey Wright
Kyle Lohse	

The Gold Group pitchers—37 starters, 11 relievers and two pitchers who switched back and forth between bullpen and starting—accounted for 17 of the 20 Cy Young Awards in the years 2002 through 2011. The Blue Group—15 starters, 5 relievers and five pitchers who were used in both roles—pitched more seasons in the majors (per pitcher) than the Gold Group (9.32 to 8.26) but accounted for no Cy Young Awards.

It goes without saying that, if you set aside the Gold Group pitchers, you could not identify another group of 50 major league starters who had remotely comparable success in the years 2002 to 2011. It is equally true that if you set aside the Blue Group, you also could not find another, equal group of pitchers who hung around as long, pitched as much, and accomplished as little. This is how that group was defined.

The Gold Group pitchers made an average of 177 starts and 118 relief appearances in the ten years of the study. The Blue Group pitchers made an average of 150 starts and 208 relief appearances. The Gold Group pitchers had a winning percentage of .598, and an ERA of 3.47. The Blue Group pitchers had a winning percentage of .481, and an ERA of 4.51.

The Gold Group had 3,018 Saves in 5,920 relief appearances. The Blue Group had 347 Saves in 5,194 relief appearances.

Let's look at the "out rates" of these two groups of pitchers.

Since 2002, Baseball Info Solutions has maintained charts of the outs recorded by each major league pitcher. Occasionally they miss a play because it isn't broadcast anywhere, but they get something more than 99.5% of them. An out can be one of five things:

1) A strikeout,
2) A ground ball,
3) A line drive,
4) A fly ball,
5) A pop up, or
6) Other.

I am rather curious about what "other" entails. I have thought about this a lot, since it took me about 30 hours of research to do this damned study

a) a batter stepping out of the batter's box while hitting the pitch, or

b) some sort of interference call in which the ball is not put in play and there is no strikeout.

In more than 90,000 innings of pitching in this study there were a total of 36 "other" outs, or one for each 2,500 innings, so they're not statistically significant, but I'd still like to know what they are.

Anyway, whether or not I am totally off base in my dislike of ground ball pitchers depends on how you look at the data. One way to look at it—and what I think is actually the best way to look at it—is to "rate" ground ball tendencies simply by the percentage of the pitcher's outs that were by way of the ground ball. Roy Halladay in 2010 got out 700 hitters:

> 219 by strikeout
> 280 by ground ball
> 20 by line drive
> 139 by fly ball
> 42 by pop out

700 batters retired, 280 of them by ground ball; that's a ground ball percentage of 40%. I think that's the *best* way to look at it.

Looked at in that way, it *is* true that the Ground Ball Rates of mediocre pitchers are significantly higher than the Ground Ball Rates of good pitchers. (Conversely stated, the Ground Ball Rates of good pitchers are LOWER, not higher, than the Ground Ball Rates of mediocre pitchers.)

These are the Ground Ball Rates of the 50 best pitchers in major league baseball, 2002-2011, with Ground Ball Rates figured in this way:

First	Last	Outs	SO	GB	Lin O	Fly O	PO	Other	Ground Ball Rate
Derek	Lowe	5465	1286	2926	142	909	202	0	.535
Brandon	Webb	3584	1062	1834	99	483	106	0	.512
Tim	Hudson	5236	1214	2601	154	974	293	0	.497
Greg	Maddux	4020	847	1910	136	879	248	0	.475
Roy	Halladay	6058	1697	2707	195	1063	396	0	.447
Chris	Carpenter	3851	1115	1570	116	828	221	1	.408
Felix	Hernandez	3791	1251	1537	87	728	188	0	.405
Mark	Buehrle	5931	1231	2354	215	1534	596	1	.397
Mariano	Rivera	1876	633	725	58	280	180	0	.386
Andy	Pettite	4350	1252	1655	161	959	320	3	.380
Roy	Oswalt	5537	1615	2078	159	1199	486	0	.375
Adam	Wainwright	2405	721	896	65	528	194	1	.373
Carlos	Zambrano	4975	1531	1804	135	1089	416	0	.363
Josh	Johnson	2005	665	704	62	432	142	0	.351
John	Lackey	5162	1451	1799	157	1325	430	0	.349
Roger	Clemens	2869	951	994	75	650	199	0	.346
Jon	Lester	2605	893	892	73	548	197	2	.342
John	Smoltz	2802	926	954	61	661	200	0	.340
Jason	Isringhausen	1295	422	437	32	294	110	0	.337

First	Last	Outs	SO	GB	Lin O	Fly O	PO	Other	Ground Ball Rate
Jamie	Moyer	4784	1023	1608	146	1419	586	2	.336
Mike	Mussina	3658	1063	1225	123	940	306	1	.335
Dan	Haren	4763	1435	1593	119	1228	388	0	.334
CC	Sabathia	5995	1841	2005	194	1418	535	2	.334
Bartolo	Colon	3666	942	1203	117	1028	376	0	.328
Josh	Beckett	4761	1594	1535	108	1106	422	1	.322
Cole	Hamels	3249	1090	1046	83	731	298	1	.322
Tim	Lincecum	2890	1122	918	49	636	165	0	.318
Randy	Wolf	4491	1235	1370	151	1247	487	1	.305
Jake	Peavy	4442	1549	1308	128	1031	424	2	.294
Francisco	Cordero	1915	694	561	51	464	145	0	.293
Cliff	Lee	4535	1320	1320	117	1342	435	1	.291
Matt	Cain	3715	1080	1070	80	1099	386	0	.288
Randy	Johnson	3887	1462	1119	108	879	324	0	.288
Javier	Vazquez	5828	1877	1667	156	1530	593	0	.286
Clayton	Kershaw	1972	742	558	47	424	201	0	.283
Curt	Schilling	3116	1083	877	80	763	313	0	.281
Justin	Verlander	3677	1213	1029	82	1013	340	0	.280
Pedro	Martinez	3206	1170	889	73	781	292	1	.277
Joakim	Soria	891	341	241	25	216	68	0	.270
Jason	Schmidt	2986	1036	790	65	801	294	0	.265
Johan	Santana	5025	1783	1313	118	1283	527	1	.261
Ted	Lilly	4987	1477	1299	144	1404	662	1	.260
Francisco	Rodriguez	1830	803	467	40	376	144	0	.255
Jose	Valverde	1487	600	373	31	322	161	0	.251
Trevor	Hoffman	1279	405	315	23	392	144	0	.246
Jered	Weaver	3199	974	784	67	965	409	0	.245
Billy	Wagner	1581	693	387	36	340	125	0	.245
Joe	Nathan	1574	646	371	28	364	165	0	.236
Jonathan	Papelbon	1239	509	292	28	275	135	0	.236
Eric	Gagne	1027	484	241	30	187	91	0	.235

These pitchers retired an average of 32.8% of hitters by Ground Balls, and only 6 of the 50 pitchers—12%—had Ground Ball rates over 40%.

These, on the other hand, are the Ground Ball Rates of the 25 pitchers in the Blue Group:

First	Last	Outs	SO	GB	Lin O	Fly O	PO	Other	Ground Ball Rate
Aaron	Cook	3490	558	1921	112	689	210	0	.550
Jamey	Wright	2432	546	1167	71	503	145	0	.480
Carlos	Silva	3347	553	1509	110	912	263	0	.451
Jason	Marquis	4146	856	1860	101	1056	272	1	.449
Jeff	Suppan	4419	877	1825	127	1189	399	2	.413
Miguel	Batista	3736	859	1540	107	915	314	1	.412
Jeremy	Affeldt	2003	577	793	53	439	141	0	.396
Nate	Robertson	3101	773	1194	81	795	258	0	.385
Mark	Hendrickson	3166	664	1217	111	853	320	1	.384
Josh	Fogg	3116	610	1182	97	918	309	0	.379
LaTroy	Hawkins	1663	443	614	63	417	126	0	.369
Brett	Tomko	3281	737	1194	92	911	345	2	.364
Jeremy	Bonderman	3233	925	1163	71	827	246	1	.360
Jose	Contreras	3209	867	1148	99	785	310	0	.358
David	Weathers	1643	439	586	45	435	137	1	.357
Rodrigo	Lopez	3653	845	1301	122	1050	334	1	.356
Kyle	Lohse	4614	1031	1635	131	1371	443	3	.354
Doug	Davis	3874	1092	1365	121	938	358	0	.352
Jeff	Weaver	3449	809	1179	106	962	392	1	.342
Ryan	Franklin	3050	600	1011	95	957	387	0	.331
Gil	Meche	3484	942	1123	91	1005	323	0	.322
Guillermo	Mota	1955	589	625	50	508	183	0	.320
Scott	Linebrink	1744	548	458	55	500	183	0	.263
Kyle	Fransworth	1691	637	433	57	409	155	0	.256
Oliver	Perez	3103	1121	658	72	898	354	0	.212

These pitchers recorded an average of 36.9% of their batter outs by way of the ground ball, and 6 of the 25—24%—were over 40%.

The reason the percentage is higher for the Blue Group than for the Gold Group, however, is simply strikeouts. We can also state the ground ball tendencies of the pitchers as a Ground Ball/Fly Ball Ratio. If we do that, then the Ground Ball Ratios of the Gold Group are actually higher than the Ground Ball Ratios of the Blue Group:

While these are the Ground Ball Ratios of the Blue Group:

First	Last	GB	Fly Out	Pop Out	Ground Ball Ratio
Brandon	Webb	1834	483	106	3.11 - 1
Derek	Lowe	2926	909	202	2.63 - 1
Tim	Hudson	2601	974	293	2.05 - 1
Roy	Halladay	2707	1063	396	1.86 - 1
Greg	Maddux	1910	879	248	1.69 - 1
Felix	Hernandez	1537	728	188	1.68 - 1
Mariano	Rivera	725	280	180	1.58 - 1
Chris	Carpenter	1570	828	221	1.50 - 1
Andy	Pettitte	1655	959	320	1.29 - 1
Adam	Wainwright	896	528	194	1.24 - 1
Roy	Oswalt	2078	1199	486	1.23 - 1
Josh	Johnson	704	432	142	1.23 - 1
Carlos	Zambrano	1804	1089	416	1.20 - 1
Jon	Lester	892	548	197	1.20 - 1
Roger	Clemens	994	650	199	1.17 - 1
Tim	Lincecum	918	636	165	1.15 - 1
John	Smoltz	954	661	200	1.11 - 1
Mark	Buehrle	2354	1534	596	1.11 - 1
Jason	Isringhausen	437	294	110	1.08 - 1
CC	Sabathia	2005	1418	535	1.03 - 1
John	Lackey	1799	1325	430	1.03 - 1
Cole	Hamels	1046	731	298	1.02 - 1
Josh	Beckett	1535	1106	422	1.00 - 1
Dan	Haren	1593	1228	388	0.99 - 1
Mike	Mussina	1225	940	306	0.98 - 1
Randy	Johnson	1119	879	324	0.93 - 1
Francisco	Cordero	561	464	145	0.92 - 1
Jake	Peavy	1308	1031	424	0.90 - 1
Francisco	Rodriquez	467	376	144	0.90 - 1
Clayton	Kershaw	558	424	201	0.89 - 1
Eric	Gagne	241	187	91	0.87 - 1
Bartolo	Colon	1203	1028	376	0.86 - 1

First	Last	GB	Fly Out	Pop Out	Ground Ball Ratio
Joakim	Soria	241	216	68	0.85 - 1
Billy	Wagner	387	340	125	0.83 - 1
Pedro	Martinez	889	781	292	0.83 - 1
Curt	Schilling	877	763	313	0.82 - 1
Jamie	Moyer	1608	1419	586	0.80 - 1
Randy	Wolf	1370	1247	487	0.79 - 1
Javier	Vazquez	1667	1530	593	0.79 - 1
Jose	Valverde	373	322	161	0.77 - 1
Justin	Verlander	1029	1013	340	0.76 - 1
Cliff	Lee	1320	1342	435	0.74 - 1
Johan	Santana	1313	1283	527	0.73 - 1
Jason	Schmidt	790	801	294	0.72 - 1
Matt	Cain	1070	1099	386	0.72 - 1
Jonathan	Papelbon	292	275	135	0.71 - 1
Joe	Nathan	371	364	165	0.70 - 1
Ted	Lilly	1299	1404	662	0.63 - 1
Trevor	Hoffman	315	392	144	0.59 - 1
Jered	Weaver	784	965	409	0.57 - 1

The Gold Group averages 1.095 to 1; the Blue Group, 1.080 to 1.

So what do we conclude? Well...I still don't really like ground ball pitchers, but I do concede that I was, in the past, too radical in my distrust of them. I think that the advantages of throwing ground balls have been horribly overstated and that the best way to get batters out is to find pitchers who can throw high fastballs. However, throwing ground balls does appear to be a small advantage for the pitcher, if you control for the number of strikeouts. Given two pitchers with the same strikeout rate and the same walk rate, it does appear that we should favor the one who gets more ground balls, although this advantage is probably no larger than the advantage of being a good fielding pitcher or the advantage of having a good move to first.

To clear up a couple of points:

a) When I talk about ground ball pitchers getting hurt, I'm not really talking about guys like Adam Wainwright and Andy Pettitte, with Ground Ball Rates around 38% or Ground Ball/Fly Ball Ratios around 5 to 4. In that context, I was talking about the guys with really extreme ground ball tendencies, like Chien-Ming Wang and Brandon Webb. Those guys, it seems to me, *always* self-destruct after a couple of years, unless their name is spelled "D-e-r-e-k-L-o-w-e". I don't know why.

b) In the preamble ramble, I made the statement that 80% of the best pitchers are fly ball pitchers. That's too extreme a statement; it doesn't stand up to the evidence. We *could* say accurately that 80% of the best pitchers are not ground ball pitchers, defining a ground ball pitcher as "any pitcher with a Ground Ball/Fly Ball Ratio of 3-2, or a Ground Ball Out Percentage above 40% or even very near 40%."

c) To say that "there are no fish there" is not accurate.

d) However, many of the statements which have been made by sabermetric *advocates* of ground ball pitchers are also inaccurate. But I will leave it for them to clean up their own messes.

———•———

Jumping the Fictional Shark

by Bill James

———

It is within human nature, I think, to become less interested in fiction as we age. I'm 64; I don't read much fiction any more. I find that a lot of people in my age cadre don't. Some do; my sister, who is 75 and has limited mobility due to a stroke, still reads a couple of novels a week and has for 60 years; it becomes increasingly difficult for her to recognize the stuff she has already read.

But a lot of us lose interest in fiction as we age, and by "fiction" I mean to include movies and sit coms and stuff that tells made-up stories. When we were young we would watch anything on television. The entire nation in the 1960s watched shows like *Bewitched* and *Gilligan's Island*—shows that seem now preposterously simplistic. They had audiences in their day in the tens of millions. *Green Acres*. Grown-ups watched *Green Acres* and *Hogan's Heroes* and laughed at the jokes.

I can pinpoint a few moments in my life at which this pleasure fled from me. When I got out of the Army in 1973 I didn't want to do anything except get myself a room and lie on the bed and watch television. In the Army people tell you what to do about 120 hours a week. Some people are comfortable with that; some people stay in the Army because they need somebody else to structure their lives. Some people get out of prison and have to get back in because they can't live unstructured lives. I'd have killed myself if I couldn't get out of the Army after a couple of years. Having somebody tell me what to do all the time was hell to me. I just wanted to NOT DO ANYTHING for a while.

I got myself a cheap room and a little black-and-white TV, which by the way still works; this was 40 years ago. It took me about two weeks before I was ready to get up and engage the world again, but it didn't take nearly that long for the TV to grow tiresome. Between 1971 and 1973, in my view, television had turned to mush. I couldn't believe how bad the shows were. CBS had cancelled, in the words of Pat Buttram, "every show that had a tree in it." It must have been...oh, I don't know; November 5, 1973. I've never felt the same about television since.

When my wife and I were first married there were shows we would watch, fictional shows; we'd watch *Barney Miller* and *Cheers*, a few others. I can pinpoint the moment at which they lost us. We used to watch the show *L.A. Law*. About the third year of *L.A. Law* there was an episode in which Harry Hamlin, who played a lawyer, was cross-examining a policeman during a deposition about a shooting, and the cop was saying, "What would you do, if you were in this situation, where a punk was pointing a gun in your face and you had to decide in the matter of a second whether he was going to live or you were, what would you do?"

"I don't know," said Hamlin, "I've never faced that situation."

"Well, face it now," says the cop, and he pulls his gun and points it in Hamlin's face. It was a very dramatic moment, and we gasped, and then they cut to a commercial.

And when they came back from the commercial, they had just dropped the whole thing; the cop had put his weapon away, and the deposition had ended and the show had moved on. Their message to their viewers was, "We control this experience; we can manipulate you to think what we want you to think, and then we can move on however we want to move on." That's right, you can—but we're done. We lost interest in the show after that, because...well, it was just a show. They had demonstrated too forcefully that they could do whatever they wanted to with the show. Without parameters it was just play-acting.

In a sense the show had jumped the shark; we have that expression for that now, which we didn't then. In a sense the show had jumped the shark, but the transition was more profound than that. It wasn't that the show had changed but that we had changed; we had surrendered our disbelief for the last time. We had gotten too old for television; I guess I was 35.

Sometimes old people talk about how things aren't the way they used to be; politics used to be civil, and marriage used to be a real commitment, and things used to be built to last, and athletes used to care about their fans, and businessmen used to be honest, and people didn't file lawsuits because their coffee was too hot, and things used to be made in America, and we didn't used to have beggars all over the streets, and TV shows used to have trees in them.

Some of this is real; the world *does* change, and some things aren't what they once were, and some of the changes are for the worse, although more of them are for the better. Television grows constantly more sophisticated in an effort to hold on to an ever-evaporating audience. A lot of it is just...well, stuff wears out on you. The magic doesn't work anymore. I am not any less interested in the world than I used to be, but as I grow older I am more interested in the world that really is, rather than in the stuff that people make up to try to entertain me.

———•———

Mindless Education

by Bill James

There is this education debate going on; it has to do with K through 12. American kids, we are told by the same savant who seven years ago was telling us that Florida was about to be buried under the Atlantic ocean, are now 21st in the world in math skills, and 25th in science, whereas a generation ago we were #1 in both areas.

I am not saying that this is untrue, but...I am skeptical about it on a great many different levels. First of all, I'm an old person, and I actually *remember* what people were saying about the American education system way back when, which actually was pretty much the same thing they are saying now. Remember "Why Johnny Can't Read?"...anybody remember that? Why Johnny Can't Add; Why Johnny Doesn't Know History?

Oh yes, our schools from the 1950s and 1960s were terrible; the Russians were far better than we were, the Germans were better, the Japanese were better. The current generation of Why-Johnny-Can't-Read alarmists sound, to me, a great deal like the last generation. I've been hearing this for a long time; I always wonder what the specifics are. What exactly is being tested here?

This is not to say that it's not true; if you run around saying every day that Grandma is going to die tomorrow, the fact that you were wrong yesterday doesn't mean that you are wrong today or that you will be wrong tomorrow. But if you were told that American kids a generation ago were 1st in the world in math skills, but now they are 21st among 30 developed nations, what would be the first question you would ask?

Is this because American kids are doing worse, or is it because kids from other countries are doing better?

Of course it makes a difference. All of life is not a mindless

103

competition. If our kids have improved by 10% but those from other nations have improved by 30%, that's one problem. If our kids have actually gone backward, that's a different problem.

If other countries' educational systems have improved dramatically then we should begin, I think, by celebrating the fact that other countries are doing better than they were. That's a good thing. We will all benefit from that.

Maybe it's just me, but...my kids

a) have worked far, far harder in school than I ever did, and
b) are far better educated than I was at the same age.

I *don't* think it's just me. I know that when I have written things like this in the past, I always hear from teachers who say "That's right; the kids *do* work much harder now than they did a generation ago. The standards are much higher."

Look, here is what I think is happening; maybe I'm wrong, I'm not an expert. What I think is happening is not that we're doing a poor job of educating our kids, but that we're doing a very poor job of selling our kids on the *value* of education. Many, many more young people go to college now than did when I graduated from high school, but there is this difference. When I got out of high school, the smart kids wanted to go to college because we wanted to get ahead in life. Now, the kids from good families are all going to go to college because it's expected of them.

What I am concerned about is that there is too much "push" in our educational system, and not enough "pull." It's not that we're not pushing the kids hard enough; rather, we are beginning to push them too hard, and it is time to BACK OFF. High school kids now work really hard, and a good bit of it is just busy work. They *are* better educated, as a group, than we were; but they are also doing a lot of work-for-the-purpose-of-work. In fact, in a lot of families, the kids are now working harder than the parents are.

Well, what do you think is going to happen if the kids decide that they're working harder than their parents are? I can tell you what's going to happen, if it's not obvious to you. They're going to rebel. They're going to start refusing to do it. Maybe they've already started refusing to do it, I don't know.

There's a different problem that is related. We have pockets in our society, pockets of poverty, which are perpetuated by the fact that people don't believe that they can get out of poverty by working hard and getting an education. I was raised in poverty, and I mean *true* poverty; as I'm sure I've mentioned, my father was a small-town school janitor, and we didn't have plumbing or television or heated bedrooms. But I always *expected* to do better, and I always saw education as the way to do better. There are pockets of poverty now—black and white—where people don't get that anymore.

But we are also reaching a point, I think, of mindless education; it's an oxymoron, but I kind of think it's where we are. We're pushing our kids to get more education and more education and more education, but we're not really explaining to them *why*, and we're not explaining to them why because we can't explain to them *why*, and we can't explain to them why because there isn't any *why* there; it's just education for the purpose of education. We're pushing kids to get Master's Degrees because the Bachelor's doesn't do it anymore; you have to have an advanced degree now and you have to do better in school because the Chinese are doing better in school, and there's some sort of obscure competition between us and they're going to win.

Pardon me for being dense, but I don't see what difference it makes how the Chinese kids are doing on their math tests. So what? Do you *really* think that we're going to become a third-world nation because the Chinese kids are doing better on their math tests? Why? Explain it to me, as if I was an idiot. I don't get the connection. I don't see what difference it makes. Cutting-edge scientists, yes, but that's a different problem. Owing trillions of dollars to the Chinese because we're spending money we don't need to spend is a serious problem that will impact the lives of Americans if we don't stop it. But education is not an Olympic competition; in fact, it's not a competition at all. Falling behind in some imaginary competition is not a serious problem, and please stop assuming that it is.

And stop telling the kids to work harder; it's backfiring on us, and it's making the problem worse. If Japanese kids go to school 244 days a year or whatever it is supposed to be, then frankly the Japanese should be ashamed of themselves. You remember what Bill Russell said when the East German women were winning all of the swimming medals because they took male hormones and ate steroids like candy? He said let them. At that point, he said, you let them have it; it's just a medal. If the Japanese want to go to school year around, let them. All they're gaining is a medal. What they're losing is their childhood.

———•———

THE STANDARDS OF A HALL OF FAME MANAGER

by Bill James

Let us begin with the question of "How many Hall of Fame managers should there be?" Or, if you prefer, "How many managers should be in the Hall of Fame?"

Of position players who played in the 1920s (1920 to 1929), 11.0% are in the Hall of Fame, unless the Hall of Fame has recently elected some yahoo for whom I failed to account; from the 1950s, 7.3%. Those are numbers based on seasons, rather than at bats or careers; in other words, Hall of Fame players account for 7.3% of all player/seasons in the 1950s. Those numbers, however, include players with only a few at bats. Since a manager is the *most* regular of the regular "players," the more relevant percentage would probably be for regulars. For players with 400 plate appearances, the percentages are 24% from the 1920s and 17% from the 1950s.

So we could begin, then, with the assumption that Hall of Fame managers should account for no more than 25% of teams managed; you can argue for less, but can we agree that it shouldn't be over 25%? Through 2013 there have been 2,696 major league team/seasons, depending on what you count. Hall of Fame recognition lags behind performance, however, so let's back that up about ten years, and the number would be 2,396.

Hall of Fame managers, then, should account for no more than about 600 team/seasons. A couple of qualifications here. I'm not going to count Hall of Fame *players* who also managed, like Walter Johnson and Ted Williams. A few guys, like Cap Anson and Fred Clarke, we'll count them half as players and half as managers, and, by the same logic, we'll count Connie Mack half as a manager and half as an owner.

Let's look at the guys who are in the Hall of Fame.

Name	YEARS	GAMES
John McGraw	33	4769
Joe McCarthy	24	3487
Connie Mack	53	7755
Walter Alston	23	3658
Sparky Anderson	26	4030
Casey Stengel	25	3766
Fred Clarke	19	2829
Miller Huggins	17	2570
Earl Weaver	17	2541
Leo Durocher	24	3739
Frank Selee	16	2180
Bill McKechnie	25	3647
Cap Anson	21	2288
Al Lopez	17	2425
Tommy Lasorda	21	3050
Billy Southworth	13	1770
Ned Hanlon	19	2530
Dick Williams	22	3023
Bucky Harris	29	4408
Whitey Herzog	19	2409
Harry Wright	18	1825
Wilbert Robinson	19	2819

Hall of Fame managers managed 500 seasons or partial seasons, and managed 71,518 games. But we are treating Cap Anson and Cap Clarke half as players (Fred Clarke was in fact called "Cap") and Connie Mack half as an owner, which adjusts their numbers, and would make the totals 453 seasons and 65,083 games. If we treat each 150 games as a season, that's 434 seasons worth of Hall of Fame managing.

We can reach, then, this early if somewhat unpersuasive conclusion: *The number of managers in the Hall of Fame is consistent with the number of Hall of Fame players and is not unreasonable.*

Unpersuasive, however, for this reason. Through baseball history a very large number of teams have been managed by people who are in the Hall of Fame but not on our list of Hall of Fame managers. Branch Rickey, for example, managed 1,277 major league games and is in the Hall of Fame, but not as a manager. Edward Barrow managed 639 games and is in the Hall of Fame, but not as a manager.

More troubling than those are, for example, Charlie Comiskey and Clark Griffith, who were not only managers but very, very good managers with fairly long careers, but who are listed on the Hall of Fame rosters as "Pioneers" and "Executives" when they might equally well be listed as managers. The percentage of all teams which are managed by Hall of Fame managers turns out to be surprisingly difficult to establish...but moving on.

What accomplishments are relevant to Hall of Fame standing? With exceptions and limitations that will be discussed in a moment, there would appear to be only five:

  a) Winning games,
  b) Winning a high percentage of your games,
  c) Winning championships,
  d) Winning the World Series, and
  e) Having teams that exceed reasonable expectations.

Exceptions and limitations. A manager could also be historically significant as an innovator, as a personality, a leader, a pathfinder, or as a developer of talent.

It is however, difficult to see that any of those things has ever led to the selection of anyone as a Hall of Fame manager, with the exceptions of Rube Foster and Harry Wright, and it is difficult to see that these things *should* make a Hall of Fame manager. As a personality...well, you can't have any more personality than Casey Stengel, but if he hadn't won big with the Yankees, would that make him a Hall of Famer? Doug Rader had a HUGE personality, but he didn't win.

As a developer of talent...let us say that Davey Johnson deserves some of the credit for the early-career success of Doc Gooden. What Johnson did with Gooden was unusual. At the age of 18, Gooden in the minors was 19-4 with 300 strikeouts in 191 innings. Most people, however, were cautioning *against* moving Gooden too fast, talking about giving him at least 15 or 20 starts at Double A and some time in the bullpen before he went into the major league rotation. Johnson basically said, "No way in hell; he is better than my other pitchers, and he's going into my rotation. Now." Not a direct quote; a characterization of his statements and actions at that time.

Johnson deserves credit for that decision, without which Dwight Gooden would probably have wasted his best seasons in the minor leagues, as some young pitchers do. But is this separate and distinct credit for Davey Johnson, or is it an element of his other credentials? Because Johnson did this, the Mets won 90 games in 1984, 98 games in 1985, and 108 games and a World Championship in 1986. *That* is what Johnson accomplished.

Look at it this way: Who was Walter Johnson's first major league manager? Who was Bob Gibson's first major league manager? Who was Bob Feller's first major league manager? Who was Cy Young's first major league manager?

Joe Cantillon, Solly Hemus, Steve O'Neill, Gus Schmelz. Are any of this men in the Hall of Fame, or should they be?

We should leave the door open a crack here. If there was a manager who consistently, over a period of time, played a key role in the development of superstar players one after another, then we should respect that and consider its weight. Perhaps the best example of that ever is Ed Barrow, who played key roles in the development of Honus Wagner, Ty Cobb, Babe Ruth, Pie Traynor, Joe DiMaggio and Mickey Mantle. But in the normal course of a career, having a 19-year-old superstar dropped into your lap is more in the nature of "extreme good fortune" than "Hall of Fame credential."

An innovator, a leader and a path-finder...obviously these definitions overlap, and in this case we should leave the door open more than a crack.

But at the same time, that's a dangerous concept. Innovation is everywhere in baseball. Innovation is what drives all changes in baseball, and every successful manager is an innovator in different ways. Herman Franks, more than any one other manager, defined the role of the modern reliever when he announced that he would protect Bruce Sutter's overworked arm by using him only to protect leads at the end of the game. Prior to Franks, relief aces (like Gossage and Fingers) were brought in to games when the team was behind but close, and were routinely brought in when the score was tied. Franks' use of Sutter was an extremely important innovation.

But does it make him a Hall of Famer, given his modest managerial record? Of course it does not. EVERYBODY is an innovator. Nobody thinks of Walter Alston as a big innovator, but he played a major role in at least three changes in the game. First, before Walter, managers would publicly criticize their players. Walter felt that it was improper for a manager to criticize his players in the newspaper, and this practice essentially spread from Walter to all other managers, becoming the accepted standard in the industry.

Second, while the usage patterns of pitchers have become steadily more regular over the entire history of baseball, they became radically more regular in the years 1959 to 1964. Walter was one of the leading managers who "regularized" pitcher usage patterns by ending the practice of flipping pitchers back and forth between starting and relieving, and keeping pitchers religiously to a starting schedule.

Third, Walter was one of the first managers to go to a five-man pitching rotation. The Dodgers were using a five-man pitching rotation by 1972, well ahead of most of baseball.

Would these things make Walter a Hall of Fame manager had he not been successful? No. Innovation is everywhere in baseball; the game changes all the time in ways that are too subtle to be documented at the time the changes are occurring, and every change results from an innovation. *Innovation does not make a great manager unless it is accompanied by success.*

The first manager to platoon players in a systematic, organized fashion was George Stallings with the Miracle Braves in 1914. But does that make Stallings a Hall of Fame manager?

Should we put Tony La Russa in the Hall of Fame because he pushed the limits on the use of left-handed relievers? Hell, to me, that's a reason to keep him out. A key concern: Did he change the game *for the better*? The constant and annoying use of more and more left-handed one-out relievers has not made the game of baseball *better*.

I guess my real point is this. If I let you start arguing that Birdie Tebbetts or Fred Hutchinson or John McNamara or Gene Mauch or Alvin Dark should be in the Hall of Fame because of his role as an innovator

a) There is going to be no end to it, ever, because innovation is everywhere in baseball, and
b) What this inevitably will lead to is paying a lot of attention to *some* innovations because they are connected to somebody's Hall of Fame brief, while ignoring other innovations which are actually more important.

Again, keep the door open a crack. If a manager really does play a key role in making baseball a *better* game, I'm open to considering that. But as a rule innovation has nothing at all to do with whether a manager belongs in the Hall of Fame.

OK, let's get back to the five things that do make a Hall of Fame manager:

a) Winning games,
b) Winning a high percentage of your games,
c) Winning championships,
d) Having teams that exceed reasonable expectations.

That's four; I decided to consolidate "winning championships" and "winning the World Series" into one category, since the World Series is a championship.

Let us say that, as a starting point, we give the manager one point for each 40 games that he won in his career. Why 40?

Don't make me explain everything; we'll be here forever. I'm trying to make 100 points a line that sort of generally separates the Hall of Famers from the lesser geniuses. One point for 40 wins is one of the decisions that makes that work.

Winning percentage…we can look at that as Wins Minus Losses. The Hall of Fame managers had 6,326 more wins than losses in their careers, this number discounting (ignoring) the negative contributions of Connie Mack and Bucky Harris, who were under .500, and also I'm ignoring Harry Wright's record in the National Association, 1871-1875, since the National Association is a bona fide major league in the same sense that Bobby Parnell is a bona fide superstar. Since there are 22 Hall of Fame Managers and we want to award around 600 points in this category, that would be one point for each 10 more Wins than Losses.

Earl Weaver won 1,480 games in his managerial career, which is 37 points. He was 420 games over .500 in his career, which 42 points. So at this point, Earl Weaver is at 79 points, which places him in a tie for seventh among the Hall of Fame managers:

Name	YEARS	Wins	Losses	Over .500	Win Points	Wins Over .500 Points	Total
John McGraw	33	2763	1948	815	69	81	150
Joe McCarthy	24	2125	1333	792	53	79	132
Connie Mack	53	3731	3948		93	0	93
Walter Alston	23	2040	1613	427	51	42	93
Sparky Anderson	26	2194	1834	360	54	36	90
Fred Clarke	19	1602	1181	421	40	42	82
Earl Weaver	17	1480	1060	420	37	42	79
Leo Durocher	24	2008	1709	299	50	29	79
Al Lopez	17	1410	1004	406	35	40	75
Frank Selee	16	1284	862	422	32	42	74
Cap Anson	21	1295	947	348	32	34	66
Bill McKechnie	25	1896	1723	173	47	17	64
Miller Huggins	17	1413	1134	279	35	27	62
Billy Southworth	13	1044	704	340	26	34	60
Tommy Lasorda	21	1599	1439	160	39	16	55

Name	YEARS	Wins	Losses	Over .500	Win Points	Wins Over .500 Points	Total
Casey Stengel	25	1905	1842	63	47	6	53
Bucky Harris	29	2158	2219		53	0	53
Dick Williams	22	1571	1451	120	39	12	51
Whitey Herzog	19	1281	1125	156	32	15	47
Ned Hanlon	19	1313	1164	149	32	14	46
Harry Wright	18	1000	825	175	25	17	42
Wilbert Robinson	19	1399	1398	1	34	0	34

The strongest Hall of Fame cases, so far in our analysis, would be for John McGraw and Joe McCarthy, and the weakest Hall of Fame managers would be Wilbert Robinson, Harry Wright, Ned Hanlon and Jersey Whitehog. It is early, but I will alert you in advance that Whitey is not going to move up very much as we study the credentials in more depth. I'm not anti-Herzog; I always liked the guy, and I'm glad they elected him. But facts are facts; records are records.

OK, next we look at winning championships. Suppose that we give 5 points for winning a Division Championship, 10 for a League Championship, 15 for a World Championship.

Way too many points. If we did that, the 22 Hall of Fame managers would earn a total of 1,400 points, or about 64 apiece. This criterion works on a different level, though. From 1903 to 1960 there would be 25 points each year (except 1904), with 16 teams each year, or 1.56 points per team. Now, there would be 45 points each year with 30 teams, or 1.50 points per year—about the same ratio. So the proportions are fine; it's just the numbers that are too high.

Let's go with three points for a Division Championship, six for a League Championship, nine for a World Championship (no doubling up; it's not nine ADDITIONAL points for the World Championship).

By that scale, the most qualified managers among the 'famers are Casey Stengel, Joe McCarthy, Connie Mack and John McGraw:

Name	Div Championships	League	World	Championship Points
Casey Stengel	0	3	7	78
Joe McCarthy	0	2	7	73
Connie Mack	0	4	5	65
John McGraw	0	7	3	62
Walter Alston	0	3	4	51
Sparky Anderson	2	2	3	43
Miller Huggins	0	3	3	42
Tommy Lasorda	4	2	2	40
Dick Williams	1	2	2	31
Earl Weaver	2	3	1	30
Fred Clarke	0	4	1	29
Bill McKechnie	0	2	2	28
Billy Southworth	0	2	2	28
Whitey Herzog	3	2	1	28
Frank Selee	0	5	0	25
Cap Anson	0	5	0	25
Ned Hanlon	0	5	0	25
Bucky Harris	0	1	2	23
Leo Durocher	0	2	1	19
Al Lopez	0	2	0	10
Harry Wright	0	2	0	10
Wilbert Robinson	0	2	0	10

When we add these points to those we had before, we get the following:

Name	Total	Name	Total
John McGraw	212	Tommy Lasorda	95
Joe McCarthy	205	Bill McKechnie	92
Connie Mack	158	Cap Anson	91
Walter Alston	144	Billy Southworth	88
Sparky Anderson	133	Al Lopez	85
Casey Stengel	131	Dick Williams	82
Fred Clarke	111	Bucky Harris	76
Earl Weaver	109	Whitey Herzog	75
Miller Huggins	104	Ned Hanlon	71
Frank Selee	99	Harry Wright	52
Leo Durocher	98	Wilbert Robinson	44

And finally, we have Performance Against Expectation. The Baltimore Orioles didn't win their league in 2012, or their division, or the World Series—but they certainly won a great many more games than anyone expected them to win. We have to give Buck Showalter some credit for that. How do we do that?

I have a formula, and a file that has the relevant information in it. The formula is for "Expected Wins in a Season"—expected wins by a team, given their won-lost record in recent seasons. A team's expected winning percentage in 2013 was:

One times their won-lost record in 2011, plus
Two times their won-lost record in 2012, plus
162 wins and 162 losses.

For example, for the Baltimore Orioles in 2012, their won-lost record in 2010 was 66-96.

Won-Lost Record in 2010:	66	96

Their won-lost record in 2011 was 69-93. Two times that is 138-186:

Won-Lost Record in 2010:	66	96
Two Times their Won-Lost Record in 2011:	138	186

To this we add 162 wins and 162 losses, giving them an expected winning percentage in 2012 of .452, so their expected won-lost record in 2012 was 73-89:

Won-Lost Record in 2010:	66	96
Two Times their Won-Lost Record in 2011:	138	186
Tendency to Drift to the Center	162	162
Total	366	444
Winning Percentage	.452	
Expected Won-Lost Record in 2012:	73	89

The formula works, on average; teams that are expected to finish 73-89, on average, will finish 73-89. The 2012 Orioles did twenty games better than that; they finished 93-69. That makes Buck Showalter +20 games in 2012. +20 is a good year. There are 68 teams in baseball history that are +20 or better.

(For expansion teams, we assume they are coming off two consecutive seasons with records of 54-108, which makes the expectation for a first-year expansion team 65-97, and then of course you have to adjust expectations for everybody else in the league. For teams before 1961 we use 154-154 rather than 162-162, for obvious reasons.)

Anyway, I have a file which has these expectations and plusses and minuses for everybody. These numbers are kind of interesting, so let's dwell on them a little bit. Billy Martin had nine seasons in his career in which his team exceeded expectations by at least five games. His 1974 Texas Rangers (83-76) exceeded expectations by 18 games; they had lost 105 games the previous season. His 1980 Oakland A's (83-79) exceeded expectations by 15 games, as did his 1969 Minnesota Twins (97-65) and his 1976 New York Yankees (97-62). The 1981 Oakland A's were +13, the 1985 Yankees +12, the 1977 Yankees +11, the 1983 Yankees +10, and the 1971 Detroit Tigers +9.

That's a very impressive record; those nine teams exceeded expectations by a total of 117 games (it adds up to 118, but I'm using an extra decimal behind the scenes.) That's a very impressive total, but is nowhere near a record. Bill McKechnie had thirteen overperforming teams which exceeded expectations by 139 games. Bobby Cox had 16 overperforming teams that exceeded expectations by 185 games. Connie Mack, while he also had many desultory seasons, had 18 teams that exceeded expectations by a total of 234 games, which is the record. Davey Johnson is +129 games with ten teams. Fred Clarke was +121 games with 9 teams. Joe McCarthy was +187 games with 16 teams. John McGraw was +227 games with 18 overperforming teams. Leo Durocher was +164 with 12 teams. Miller Huggins was +131 with 9 teams. Sparky Anderson was +133 with 12 teams.

Billy Martin's teams added more wins than some of these other managers, but in looking at it that way, Martin is taking advantage of the low expectations for those teams. He had several teams that were coming off of dreadful seasons and did well.

That's impressive—but is it *more* impressive than sustaining excellence? Not by this method. By this method, if you've been losing 100 games a year, you're expected to lose 92, but if you've been winning 100 games a year, you're expected to win 92. If you can continue to win 100 games a year, you're outperforming expectations.

Anyway...accounting. Here's what I did. First, I ignored any seasons in which teams outperformed expectations by less than 5 games. Then I gave each manager:

1 point for a season in which his team outperformed expectations by 5 to 9 games,

2 points for a season in which his team exceeded expectations by 10 to 14 games,

3 points for 15 to 19 games,

4 points for 20 to 24 games,

5 points for 25 to 29 games,

Etc.

Billy Martin earned 21 points in his career because his teams in 9 different seasons did substantially better than expected. This is the tenth highest total of all time.

OK, let's add these points to the totals we had before for the Hall of Fame managers, and see what we've got:

Manager	Previous Total	Overperforming Teams	New Total
John McGraw	212	38	250
Joe McCarthy	205	32	237
Connie Mack	158	39	197
Walter Alston	144	17	161
Sparky Anderson	133	22	155
Casey Stengel	131	14	145
Fred Clarke	111	20	131
Leo Durocher	98	30	128
Earl Weaver	109	17	126
Miller Huggins	104	22	126
Frank Selee	99	18	117
Bill McKechnie	92	21	113
Tommy Lasorda	95	15	110
Cap Anson	91	18	109
Billy Southworth	88	14	102
Al Lopez	85	15	100
Dick Williams	82	15	97
Bucky Harris	76	19	95
Ned Hanlon	71	21	92
Whitey Herzog	75	13	88
Harry Wright	52	16	68
Wilbert Robinson	44	14	58

Wilbert Robinson's election to the Hall of Fame, I think it may be said, was a capricious selection not justified by his record as a manager.

Harry Wright...well, we can give him a little extra credit for inventing professional baseball.

Whitey Herzog, as much as I like him, may not fully meet the standards of a Hall of Fame manager based solely on the record of his accomplishments.

The real purpose of this exercise, of course, is to allow us to compare the records of other managers who are Hall of Fame candidates to those of the managers who have been selected to the Hall of Fame.

I get questions all the time: What do you think of the Hall of Fame candidacy of Bruce Bochy, of Gene Mauch, of Davey Johnson, of Charlie Manuel? A short while ago, I didn't have any method to address those questions. Now I do.

What we have essentially done here is to take all of the things that managers do and pound them into one dimension. We've taken the Wins, Losses, Winning Percentage, Championships won and record of teams exceeding expectations and stated all of that along a common scale to enable us to compare the credentials of a Hall of Fame candidate with those of the managers actually selected to the Hall of Fame. For Hall of Fame candidates, let's go back to the 1950s, and start there. I'll list the managers by date of birth.

Group One—The 1950s

Burt Shotton as a player was a rail-thin leadoff man in the Dead Ball era who would draw 100 walks a year and steal 40 bases. He played for Branch Rickey in St. Louis in the 1920s, and Rickey liked him. Shotton managed those Phillies teams in the late 1920s/early 1930s which had ridiculous hitting totals with Chuck Klein, Lefty O'Doul and Don Hurst but no pitching; he did manage to win 71 games with the Phillies in 1929 and 78 in 1932, and those were the two best seasons that the Phillies had between 1918 and 1948. They generally would lose 105.

When Leo Durocher was suspended by the Commissioner in 1947, Rickey hired Shotton to manage the Dodgers, so Shotton was the manager for Jackie Robinson in Jackie's first season. The Dodgers did OK under Shotton...well, they won the pennant...and decided they could live without Leo's substandard manners, so Shotton took over for Durocher again in mid-season 1948 and managed the Dodgers to the 1949 NL championship.

Dick Young, a sportswriter/professional provocateur in the Dan Shaughnessy mold, always referred to Shotton as KOBS, which stood for "Kindly Old Burt Shotton", and Young more or less hounded Shotton from his job.

Steve O'Neill, catcher for Cleveland in the Tris Speaker era, was, as a player, a combative redhead known for getting into fights on the field and occasionally in the dugout. As a manager he was still competitive but, like Shotton, in the "likeable manager" category. He won a World Series with Detroit in 1945, actually the only World Series title for this group of seven 1950s managers.

When Shotton was fired he was replaced by **Charlie Dressen**. Dressen was regarded as very smart, but his ego was a little out of control.

Dressen got the "smart player" tag during the 1933 World Series. Cliff Bolton had hit .410 for the 1933 Senators (16 for 39) and was being used as a pinch hitter during the series. The Giant manager, Bill Terry, went to the mound to tell the pitcher to walk Bolton, but Dressen barged into the conference uninvited and told Terry that he had managed against Bolton in the minor leagues and that if you threw Bolton a breaking pitch down and away he would ground into a double play. Terry decided to gamble that Dressen knew what he was talking about; Bolton did ground into a double play, and this became a famous incident that put Dressen on the list of future managers.

Dressen managed the Cincinnati Reds for several years in the mid-1930s. The definitive story about Dressen is that one time, with his team trailing by several runs in the early innings, he yelled to his men as they left the dugout to take the field, "Hang in there, boys; I'll think of something." That was Dressen; it was all about Charlie. He managed the great Dodger teams of 1951-1953 very successfully, winning 97, 96 and 105 games, but after the 1953 season his wife insisted that he should hold out and demand a multi-year contract, as other managers had received. The Dodgers refused to give him a multi-year contract and tried to finesse the issue, but when Dressen wouldn't yield he was fired. After that he was hired to manage the Washington Senators, failed miserably, was hired to manage the Milwaukee Braves, failed there, and managed in Detroit in the mid-1960s.

Jimmy Dykes was a Good Ole Boy manager who had quite a bit of success with the White Sox in the 1930s and 1940s, staying employed there for twelve years. The White Sox hadn't been competitive in some time, and Dykes did pretty well with them. After that finally ended he was a "coach" under Connie Mack as Mack was beginning to lose his grip; Dykes was really managing the team, although Mack continued to sit in the dugout and remained officially the manager. Dykes later managed the A's, Reds, Tigers, Orioles and Indians, but never really did have a decent team to work with.

Charley Grimm, known as Jolly Cholly, was another friendly manager. He replaced Rogers Hornsby with the Cubs in August, 1932; the Cub players hated Hornsby and loved Grimm, and they spurted to the NL championship with a 37-18 record under Grimm. He won another pennant with the Cubs, in 1935, was fired in mid-1938 (when the Cubs also won, under Gabby Hartnett), came back to win another pennant in 1945, was the first manager of the Milwaukee Braves, and managed the Cubs, for a third time, in 1960.

Grimm in the 1935 World Series horribly mishandled his starting pitching—and totally got by with it, absolutely scot-free. He had three good starting pitchers, but used all three of them in one game (October 4, 1935), lost the game, and then had to start his fourth starter the next day, which he also lost. It was one of the worst blunders in World Series history, and the press completely missed it.

In spite of that, Grimm's record as a manager does have many highlights. He managed the Cubs in the era when other teams were building farm systems and Wrigley was refusing to do so, hanging on to the past as was his nature. Grimm won 100 games with the Cubs in 1935, 93 games in 1937, 98 in 1945, and won 92 with the Braves in 1953.

Paul Richards, the Wizard of Waxahachie, was a sneaky, deceptive bastard who was famous for his ability to work with pitchers; there is a recent book about him which is supposed to be very good, although I haven't read it yet. He does have a record of making *sustained* improvement with his teams in Chicago (early 1950s) and then Baltimore (late 1950s); in fact, no other manager in baseball history has been able to sustain progress in his team the way Richards did. He built both the White Sox and the Orioles from teams that had been "down" for 30 years into teams that could go head to head with the Yankees. He was able to do this in part by finding value in players that others didn't want, most notably Nellie Fox, who was small, slow and weak, but who could get 195 hits and draw 60 walks every year, and Jim Gentile, who was a wild swinger trapped in the minor leagues but drove in a lot of runs once Richards gave him the opportunity to play.

Birdie Tebbetts, famous for chirping like a bird, although that actually isn't why he was called Birdie, was a short, heavy-set catcher, a cheerful, competitive man in the same tradition as Steve

O'Neill. He never got the chance to manage a real team, but won 91 games with the Reds in 1956—by far their best season in the 1950s—and 87 with the Cleveland Indians in 1965, which was their best season of the 1960s.

Among this group of seven managers, the only one who has any kind of Hall of Fame case at all is Jolly Cholly:

Manager	Born	Managed		Wins	Losses	WS Wins	Leagues	Divisions	Plus Seasons	SCORE
Charlie Grimm	1898	1932	1960	1287	1067	0	3	0	14	86
Steve O'Neill	1891	1935	1954	1040	821	1	0	0	5	61
Charlie Dressen	1894	1934	1966	1008	973	0	2	0	9	49
Paul Richards	1908	1951	1976	923	901	0	0	0	12	37
Jimmy Dykes	1896	1934	1961	1406	1541	0	0	0	9	30
Burt Shotton	1884	1928	1950	697	764	0	2	0	7	29
Birdie Tebbetts	1912	1954	1966	748	705	0	0	0	4	26

That's not 14 Plus Seasons for Grimm; that's 14 points for plus seasons, seasons in which his team exceeded their expected winning percentage going into the season. Grimm's Hall of Fame resume is only slightly weaker than Whitey Herzog's. Essentially, none of these men should be in the Hall of Fame based on his record as a manager.

Group 2—the 1960s

Danny Murtaugh managed the Pirates to their World Championships in 1960 and 1971. Between those two he left the job twice for health reasons.

Murtaugh, a small middle infielder, was not aggressively friendly in the mold of Charlie Grimm, Birdie Tebbetts or Steve O'Neill, but he was very well liked by his players, and he had the ability to hold the respect of his team over a long period of time, which is an immensely difficult thing to do.

Bill Rigney managed the Giants after Leo Durocher and the Twins after Billy Martin. Martin and Durocher, while great managers, were screamers. After a couple of years a team gets tired of a screamer, and they'll almost always hire a "calming presence" to replace him. Rigney was a calming presence. The highlight of his career was the first two years of his tenure with the Los Angeles Angels, a 1961 expansion team. While the other expansion teams of that era lost 100 games or nearly 100 games for years and years, the Angels won 70 games their first season and then won 86 games their second. Rigney managed the Angels almost to the end of the 1960s.

Ralph Houk was from my hometown, Lawrence, Kansas. He was a Major in the Army in World War II. That's five steps up, for those of you who weren't in the Army. There's the enlisted men, which is 90% of the service or thereabouts, then there are the Second Lieutenants (the lowest officers), First Lieutenants, Captains, Majors. Major is three steps away from a General (Lieutenant Colonel, Colonel, General.) Houk participated in the Battle of the Bulge and the Battle of Bastogne, and he won a Bronze Star, a Purple Heart, and a Silver Star.

Houk had a command personality. Although he was a second- or third-string catcher with the Yankees of the 1950s, he was one of the leaders of the team, an assertive man who helped to set the expectations in the locker room—very much as Art Jorgens, the Yankees backup catcher in the 1930s, had done in his day. When Casey Stengel was pushed out after the 1960 World Series (in large part because Stengel was behind the curve on issues of race), Houk became the Yankee manager and was tremendously successful for three seasons, 1961 to 1963. That was probably the best three-year start to a manager's career in major league history; the Yankees won 309 games and two World Series.

After the 1963 season Houk resigned as manager to become the Yankee General Manager, a role for which he was frankly very ill-suited. He returned to the dugout in 1966 and managed into the mid-1980s, but never again enjoyed any real success.

Fred Hutchinson's biography parallels Houk's in some regards. Born in 1919 (as was Houk), he attended college, served in the Navy in World War II, and rose to the level of Lieutenant Commander, which is the same as a major in the Army. Like Houk, he had an air of competence and a command personality.

He also had command of his pitches—in fact, fantastic command. In 1950 he walked only 48 men in 232 innings, and you have to remember that Walk Rates in 1950 were absurdly high. The Yankees in 1950 had three pitchers who walked 118, 138, and 160 batters—and they won the pennant. Relative to his era, Fred Hutchinson may well be the greatest control pitcher in the history of baseball. He was also one of the best-hitting pitchers of all time, hitting .382 in 1939, .315 in 1946, .302 in 1947, and .326 in 1950. In his career as a hitter he had more than twice as many walks as strikeouts—I believe the best strikeout to walk ratio, for a pitcher as a batter, in the history of baseball. He won 18 games in 1946, 17 in 1950—a rather remarkable playing career for a man who lost four prime seasons to World War II.

Hutchinson got to the chance to manage the Tigers in 1952, when he was only 32 years old. He was regarded as an extremely tough manager, which in those days meant that he would knock the crap out of you if you gave him any grief. In spite of this, he was extremely well liked by his players, at least those who would talk about it. Hutchinson rarely smiled; Joe Garagiola said of him that he was a very happy man...only his face didn't know it. After the 1954 season he asked for a multi-year contract and, as Charlie Dressen had been the year before, was forced out as Detroit manager.

He returned to manage the Cardinals (1956-1958) and the Cincinnati Reds (1959-1964). In 1961 he guided the Reds to the National League pennant, their first pennant in more than 20 years; he was matched up against Ralph Houk in that series, but Houk had a much better team. A heavy smoker, Hutchinson was diagnosed with lung cancer after the 1963 season. It was widely known that he was at death's door, and, although he remained nominally the Reds' manager, he had to step aside in June, 1964. He died in November of that year, widely celebrated for his courage. Major League baseball to this day gives the Hutch Award, which is given generally to a player who deals courageously with an illness or injury.

Alvin Dark was a very, very good player, a shortstop who would hit around .300 with 20 homers, mentioned in the MVP voting in six seasons. As a manager he was tactically brilliant, but unable to meet the very high standard of interpersonal skills that managing requires. He was always suspected of being a racist ("suspected" may be a kind word). He criticized Orlando Cepeda in the press in 1961, saying that he was tired of players leading the league in home runs and RBI and not doing anything to help the team. (Yes, that definitely counts as a stupid thing to say.) He was fired after four seasons, although he had averaged 92 wins a season. His 1966 Kansas City A's team had a famous incident on an airplane when several players were apparently spending some quality time in the bathrooms with the stewardesses, and that wound up in the newspapers. He was fired the next season although the '66 A's had had their best season ever. He managed four years in Cleveland, again with some early success, then, after Dick Williams resigned following the 1973 World Series, Dark was brought back to the A's by Charley Finley, who had fired him in 1967.

The next year there were several highly-publicized fights in the Oakland locker room and a famous incident in which the team captain, Sal Bando, shouted loudly that Alvin Dark couldn't manage an F'ing meat market, only to discover that Dark was two feet behind him. In spite of this the A's won their third consecutive World Championship in 1974, then won 98 games in 1975. Dark, 91 years old, is still alive.

Gil Hodges was an immensely popular player, and was the beloved manager of the Miracle Mets of 1969.

Gene Mauch became famous as a smart guy after an incident in the minor leagues in which the team bus tried to drive through a tunnel and got wedged in the tunnel entrance. Nobody could figure out what to do until Mauch suggested that they let the air out of the tires and see if they could back out. They were able to get the bus out of the tunnel.

Mauch got the chance to manage in the majors at the age of 34, but unfortunately with a terrible team. The 1961 Phillies lost 23 games in a row, at that time the longest losing streak in the majors since 1900. Mauch, however, had the reputation of being a genius and built on that reputation by building the Phillies over the next several years into one of the league's best teams.

In 1964, of course, the Phillies had all but clinched the National League title, then collapsed and lost it in the last two weeks. I believe that Mauch got a bad rap in that situation, but we've argued about that many times and there is no point in going over it again. After 1964 the Phillies were weakened when their second-best player, Johnny Callison, flamed out early, and were constantly distracted by interminable disputes with their best player, Dick Allen. They were never able to get to the top of the league.

Mauch then took on another building project, the expansion Montreal Expos, and was able to win 73 games with them in their second season, but could never make much progress after that. Managing in Minnesota in the late 1970s, his teams were around .500, but he finally did win two American League West division championships, with the California Angels in 1982 and 1986.

After the age of 50, his wife dying of cancer and endlessly criticized for the collapse of the 1964 Phillies, Mauch got the reputation of being a sour, bitter, sarcastic man, hostile to the press, but I interviewed him several times, and he couldn't have been any nicer to me. But then, he knew that I had defended his record, and also I had written about his record in finding relief aces, which was remarkable. Time after time in his career, he took over empty bullpens and was able to find two or three absolutely outstanding relievers. Among the relievers who had excellent seasons for Mauch with no previous history of major league success: Mike Marshall, Tom Johnson, Doug Corbett, Jack Baldschun, Donnie Moore. Numerous other relievers also had big comebacks for Mauch after their careers appeared to be over.

OK, summing up. Among this group of fine managers, Ralph Houk and Danny Murtaugh, who won two World Series apiece, came closest to meeting the standards of a Hall of Fame manager, although they fell short of that standard. Murtaugh probably would be in the Hall of Fame, had he not been forced to resign every few years to recover his health.

Manager	Born	Managed		Wins	Losses	WS Wins	Leagues	Divisions	Plus Seasons	SCORE
Ralph Houk	1919	1961	1984	1619	1531	2	1	0	9	81
Danny Murtaugh	1917	1957	1976	1115	950	2	0	0	12	73
Alvin Dark	1922	1961	1977	994	954	1	1	1	8	54
Gene Mauch	1925	1960	1987	1902	2037	0	0	2	14	53
Fred Hutchinson	1919	1952	1954	830	827	0	1	0	9	35
Bill Rigney	1918	1956	1976	1239	1321	0	0	0	9	30
Gil Hodges	1924	1963	1971	660	753	1	0	0	5	20

Group Three—the 1970s

Billy Martin, of course, is one of the most colorful figures in baseball history.

Chuck Tanner was a pioneer of the "Positive Thinking" school of managing. Whatever the problem was, he attacked it with positive thinking. He took over a White Sox team that in 1970 had lost 106 games, and in two years had built them into a serious contender—absolutely a remarkable accomplishment. It was a testimony to positive thinking, Dick Allen, and riding your best pitchers like you were Hannibal and they were elephants; in 1972 Wilbur Wood was 24-17, Stan Bahnsen 21-16, and Tom Bradley 15-14. Two years later those three pitchers were 40-45, but it was fun while it lasted.

After five pretty good years in Chicago, Tanner managed the Oakland A's in 1976, then was traded to the Pittsburgh Pirates for Manny Sanguillen. It was very, very unusual for a manager to be traded for a player; in fact, I don't think I had ever heard of it before. It was a testimony to how highly Tanner was regarded at that time.

He paid it off with a World Championship for Pittsburgh in 1979, the second highlight of his career, but then his team was torn apart by a huge, ugly, players-going-to-prison type drug scandal and allegations that Tanner had knowingly allowed drug merchants into his locker room. Although he did get one more gig, he was never able to get his managerial career back on its feet.

Danny Murtaugh resigned from the Pirates for the third time after the 1971 season, and **Bill Virdon** got the job. The 1972 Pirates won 96 games and the National League East. Murtaugh returned to the dugout for the fourth time in mid-1973, but Virdon was hired to manage the Houston Astros.

Virdon as a player was an eleven-year regular, based almost entirely on his reputation as a brilliant defensive center fielder. As a manager he was also all defense all the time. He always had a couple of .220 hitters in the lineup.

Although he apparently does have some personality off the field, Bill Virdon in 81 years has never been photographed smiling. In the late 1970s and early 1980s I worked with the Hendricks brothers in Houston and spent a lot of time in Houston and know for certain that several of Virdon's players thought that his philosophy was that if you never said anything it would take people a long time to realize that you're an idiot. In spite of this, the Astros built steadily toward a better team and won the National League West in 1980, losing the playoffs to Philadelphia in what may be the greatest Championship Series ever played, ending with four consecutive extra-inning games. Virdon was let go by Houston in 1982, and he managed Montreal for a couple of years after that.

OK, this time we do have a manager with a record comparable to that of the Hall of Fame managers:

Manager	Born	Managed		Wins	Losses	WS Wins	Leagues	Divisions	Plus Seasons	SCORE
Billy Martin	1928	1969	1988	1253	1013	1	1	3	21	100
Chuck Tanner	1928	1970	1988	1352	1381	1	0	0	9	48
Bill Virdon	1931	1972	1984	995	921	0	0	2	8	45

Billy Martin is the first manager we have found whose record—not including his record of punching out strangers in bars—

would justify his selection to the Hall of Fame. He's not overwhelmingly qualified; he would rank near the bottom of the Hall of Fame group. But he's qualified.

Group Four—the 1980s

Roger Craig was a modest, understated, good-humored man, famous for saying "Hm, Baby" and for teaching his pitchers to throw the splitter.

Don Zimmer was not actually a gerbil. My favorite Don Zimmer story has to do with when Pete Rose was hired to manage the Cincinnati Reds. Everybody was sending him roses to congratulate him, and the Reds' clubhouse was just overwhelmed with hundreds and hundreds of roses. Zimmer sent him a card that said "F--- the roses; you'd better win or it's your ass, just like the rest of us."

I really never had any sense of who **John McNamara** was or what he was about, but he was certainly around a long time.

Dick Howser, robbed of what might have been a Hall of Fame playing career by an injury, was robbed of what might have been a Hall of Fame managerial career by a brain tumor.

Buck Rodgers managed Milwaukee, Montreal and California, and you probably remember him as clearly as I do.

None of these men even approached the standard of a Hall of Fame manager, although Dick Howser was making extraordinary progress until stopped by the brain tumor:

Manager	Born	Managed		Wins	Losses	WS Wins	Leagues	Divisions	Plus Seasons	SCORE
Dick Howser	1936	1980	1986	507	425	1	1	2	5	46
Don Zimmer	1931	1972	1991	885	858	0	0	1	8	35
John McNamara	1932	1969	1996	1160	1233	0	1	1	4	34
Roger Craig	1930	1978	1992	738	737	0	1	1	6	33
Buck Rodgers	1938	1980	1994	784	774	0	0	0	1	21

Group Five—the 1990s
All I have here is Tom Kelly and Jack McKeon:

Manager	Born	Managed		Wins	Losses	WS Wins	Leagues	Divisions	Plus Seasons	SCORE
Jack McKeon	1930	1973	2011	1051	990	1	0	0	10	51
Tom Kelly	1950	1986	2001	1140	1244	2	0	0	5	40

Group Six—Recent Retirees
and Managers Who Don't Have a Managing Job Right Now

This research was done before the 2014 Hall of Fame elections of Bobby Cox, Joe Torre and Tony LaRussa, but, in that my research merely shows that Cox, Torre and LaRussa all meet the standards of a Hall of Fame manager, no real adjustment—and not much comment—appears to be needed here.

Felipe Alou was regarded by those who knew him as the sharpest manager and the sharpest person that they ever knew in terms of understanding the small details of the game. He knew when the batter was going to bunt by the way he held the bat. He knew what pitch the pitcher was likely to throw; he knew where the batter was likely to hit it. He knew everybody who shied away from contact and everybody who took an extra half-second to get rid of the ball. He knew everything that any player could not do.

He didn't have great teams or phenomenal success. He won 94 games with the Expos in 1993, had the best record in baseball with the Expos at the time the 1994 season was stopped by the strike, and won 100 games with the Giants in 2003. It may be that you cannot build great teams out of small details; it may be that focusing that intensely on the small details is not as productive as some other elements of managing. But he had his moments.

Joe Torre's major league managerial career easily exceeds the Hall of Fame standard. I credit him with 177 points—in other words, 77% more than he needed to be considered a Hall of Famer.

Bobby Cox is ridiculously over-qualified for the Hall of Fame, with 206 points. By this method he ranks as the third most-successful manager of all time, behind John McGraw and Joe McCarthy.

As a minor league player, **Lou Piniella** was famous (or infamous) for his temper, and his reputation as a hothead probably kept him out of the major leagues for a couple of years. He could always hit; he hit .310 in the Carolina League in 1963, .308 at Portland in 1967, .317 in 1968. He hit .300 seven times in the major leagues, and, while he wasn't fast or showy in the field, he was a very competent fielder.

As a manager he not quite in the "loudmouth" class with Leo Durocher and Billy Martin, but he was certainly in the "take no crap" class with Fred Hutchinson, Ralph Houk, Tom Kelly and Gil Hodges.

While his record is not on the same level as Cox, Torre and La Russa, and he may have to wait a long time because he was competing with them, Piniella's record as a manager *does* meet the Hall of Fame standard. He won 90 games with the Yankees in 1986, won the World Series with the Reds in 1990, won 90 games with the Reds in 1992, won his division with the Mariners in 1995 and 1997, won 91 with the Mariners in 2000, won 116 games with the Mariners in 2001, and then won two consecutive division titles with the Cubs in 2006 and 2007. He had nine seasons in his career in which his team exceeded expectations by five games or more, and we credit him with 21 points for those seasons—the same totals as Billy Martin. He had a very, very good managerial career—better than Herzog's, better than Dick Williams, and as good as his fellow Tampa Bay native, Al Lopez.

Tony La Russa is in the same class with Cox—far, far above the practical standards of Hall of Fame selection. By this method he ranks fifth all-time, behind McGraw, McCarthy, Cox and Connie Mack. Which I think would make him the greatest manager of all time who isn't Irish, although "Cox" may be Welsh or Cornish, not sure.

Art Howe hasn't managed since 2004? You're kidding?

I always loved **Ozzie Guillen**. OK, sometimes he says stupid shit, but then, so do I. He's got about one-third of a Hall of Fame resume, and I hope he gets a chance to build on it.

As I see it, then, there are four recently retired managers who meet the historical standards of Hall of Fame selection, and three who far exceed that level:

Manager	Born	Managed		Wins	Losses	WS Wins	Leagues	Divisions	Plus Seasons	SCORE
Bobby Cox	1941	1978	2010	2504	2001	1	4	10	31	206
Tony LaRussa	1944	1979	2011	2728	2365	3	3	7	26	196
Joe Torre	1940	1977	2010	2326	1997	4	2	7	18	177
Lou Piniella	1943	1986	2010	1835	1713	1	0	5	21	102
Felipe Alou	1935	1992	2006	1033	1021	0	0	2	8	40
Ozzie Guillen	1964	2004	2012	747	710	1	0	1	5	38
Art Howe	1946	1989	2004	392	418	0	0	2	12	24

I should stress...I probably should have stressed before now... that I am not evaluating the quality of anyone's managing. I'm not really qualified to do that, and I don't do it. I'm just evaluating the record, quantifying the amount of success the manager has enjoyed. I am taking all of the things that mark "success" for a manager— wins, winning percentage, championships and seasons exceeding reasonable expectations—and putting those all into one pile. That's all I am trying to do.

Of current major league managers, I would say that there are 13 who would seem to have some credibility as Hall of Fame candidates, although there is only one who I think is a fully qualified Hall of Famer at this point. That one is **Davey Johnson**.

Davey Johnson's career as a manager has known very little other than success. In seven seasons with the Mets he won a World Series and never finished lower than second. His Mets teams exceeded expectations based on their previous records by 17 games in 1984, 16 games in 1985, 18 games in 1986, and 10 games in 1988.

With the Cincinnati Reds, Johnson had the best record in the division two times in three seasons. His teams there exceeded expectations by 10 games in 1994 and 11 in 1995.

Moving to Baltimore, Johnson finished second and first, winning 98 games in 1997. His teams there exceeded expectations by six games in 1996 and 14 games in 1997.

With the Dodgers, Johnson did have one bad year, in 1999, but then exceeded expectations by six games in 2000.

With the Nationals in 2012, his team exceeded expectations by 20 games, winning 98 games—by far their best-ever season.

Johnson has had winning percentages of .588 with the Mets, .543 with the Reds, .574 with the Orioles, .503 with the Dodgers, and .550 with the Nationals. Despite the ten-year exile, 2000 to 2011, Johnson does have a Cooperstown-worthy record.

He's the only active manager who does, but there are three other guys who are very close to that level, and then behind them there are other strong candidates. **Dusty Baker** has, in my opinion, 94% of a Hall of Fame resume.

In plain English, Dusty Baker may well be as much of an idiot as many of you claim that he is. I don't really care; it's not my problem. Good manager or bad, he has enjoyed a significant amount of success over a long period of time. He won 90 or more games with the San Francisco Giants five times, including 103 wins in 1993. He won a divisional title in Chicago and has won two more in Cincinnati.

The San Francisco Giants won 75 games in 1991 and 72 games in 1993. They added Barry Bonds that winter—and Dusty Baker. They won 103 games in 1994.

Is it unrealistic to say that that team exceeded expectations by 27 games, given that they added Barry Bonds? Sure.

But the team *did* succeed. It is not unrealistic to say that the Giants exceeded expectations by 15 games in 1997 or that the Cincinnati Reds exceeded expectations by 15 games in 2012. Dusty Baker has had nine seasons in which his teams have exceeded expectations by a total 115 wins. That's a very solid record.

Like Davey Johnson, **Jim Leyland** was out of the managing racket for several years in the heart of the steroid era; as I recall, in his case he was kicked out for smoking. No? Whatever.

As best I can measure it, Leyland is just one point behind Dusty Baker as a Hall of Fame candidate, 94 points to 93. And yes, I would rather have Jim Leyland managing my team than Dusty Baker, but that's just my opinion.

Among all of the Hall of Fame wannabes we have discussed, there are only two whose entire managerial career has been with one team: Danny Murtaugh and **Mike Scioscia**. (Some of the actual Hall of Famers were also one-team managers.)

Like Baker and Leyland, Scioscia does not have a Hall of Fame record at this time, but is very close; I have him at 91. He has time… well, he has time if he loses some weight. He is fifteen years younger than Davey Johnson (which also makes him fifteen years younger than Mick Jagger and Keith Richards). Scioscia is actually the second-youngest manager on this list of 13 active candidates, behind Terry Francona. If he can put together one more big season—and God knows he has the talent to work with—Scioscia will have a Hall of Fame record.

Charlie Manuel scores at 74 points on our charts, 74% of a Hall of Fame record. Charlie is almost one full year older than Jim Leyland. (Both were born in 1944, but Manuel at one end of the year and Leyland at the other. Dusty Baker is my age, both of us born in 1949.) After being replaced in Philadelphia by a Hall of Famer (player, not coach) in Ryne Sandberg, Charlie may never get the chance to reach the Hall of Fame.

Bruce Bochy, six years younger than Baker and I, has 68% of a Hall of Fame resume.

Terry Francona, like Bochy, has two World Series rings and has a better won-lost record, but with fewer highlights and fewer "plus win" seasons. He is four years younger than Bochy, and I estimate that his Hall of Fame career is 59% complete.

Ron Gardenhire, having a little down phase after winning 90 games like clockwork from 2002 to 2010, is at 55 points (or 55% of a Hall of Fame career.)

Buck Showalter is at 51 points.

Joe Maddon and **Ron Washington** both got late starts in the careers, and are now at 37 points and 35 points, respectively.

If you are trying to build an impressive record, managing in places like Colorado and Pittsburgh could be considered a Hurdle. **Clint Hurdle**, halfway in age between Bochy and Francona, is a good manager but has only 30% of a Hall of Fame resume.

Jim Tracy, although I think he is also a very good manager, is only at 25 points.

Manager	Born	Managed		Wins	Losses	WS Wins	Leagues	Divisions	Plus Seasons	SCORE
Davey Johnson	1943	1984	—	1286	995	1	0	5	23	108
Dusty Baker	1949	1993	—	1581	1432	0	1	5	20	94
Jim Leyland	1944	1986	—	1676	1659	1	2	4	18	93
Mike Scioscia	1958	2000	—	1155	951	1	1	5	13	91
Charlie Manuel	1944	2000	—	947	759	1	1	4	6	74
Bruce Bochy	1955	1995	—	951	975	2	1	3	15	68
Terry Francona	1959	1997	—	1029	915	2	0	0	5	59
Ron Gardenhire	1957	2002	—	932	851	0	0	6	6	55
Buck Showalter	1956	1992	—	1078	1018	0	0	1	16	51
Joe Maddon	1954	2006	—	612	573	1	0	1	7	37
Ron Washington	1952	2007	—	520	452	0	2	0	4	35
Clint Hurdle	1957	2002	—	685	798	1	0	0	5	30
Jim Tracy	1955	2001	—	856	880	0	0	1	2	25

This chart was compiled, and the comments on active managers were written, before the 2013 season, and many of these are now slightly out of date.

Thanks for reading.

———

THE LIBERAL COACH AND THE CONSERVATIVE ATHLETE

by Bill James

A good sports team elegantly combines the animating spirits of both the conservative and the liberal political paradigm. A conservative believes two things:

1) That everyone has a responsibility to take care of himself and his own circle of interest, that society works best when everybody looks out for himself and his own, and
2) In the traditional values of hard work and fidelity to the codes of the community.

Almost every successful athlete believes in these things to the core of his being, and manifests these beliefs in his daily routine.

A liberal believes:

1) That we must all care for one another, that we must all share in the responsibilities of the communities' needs, and
2) That we must be forward-looking, innovative and inclusive, and that we must break through the barriers that have been placed upon us by the fictions and prejudices of the past.

Almost every sports organization, on one level or another, is devoted to these principles. Sports teams are and have always been the most open and inclusive organizations in society, because we care more about winning than we do about anything else, and we're not going to let the prejudices of the community hold us back. This is the message of *Moneyball* as much as it is the message of *42:The Jackie Robinson Story*.

A successful sports team, then, merges the core tenets that divide society in the verbose and windy prairies of political dispute.

135

These core tenets may be seen as the four wheels of a vehicle, and then it may be seen that the power given to each tenet must be carefully kept in balance, one to another, or you will have a vehicle with a 38-inch tire on the right front and a 27-inch tire on the left rear, and very quickly you're in the ditch.

Let us reflect now on the relative structures of three things: Family, Team, Company. (Company or Business: both words have alternative meanings that are almost wholly irrelevant to the present discussion, but there is one definition of both terms that is nearly identical, and this is the meaning on which we are focused.)

As it is true that a successful team must merge the core beliefs that in another context are seen as divisive, so this is true as well of a Family, and of a Business. In a family as well, all must carry their own weight, and yet everyone must care for one another, and in a successful business as well, everyone has to buy in to the values of the group. There is this difference: that in a family there is necessarily more of an emphasis on caring for one another, and in a business there is necessarily more of an emphasis on looking out for yourself, but these are mere differences in shading, like the difference between *de-fense* and *defense*. A sports team, to succeed, must be a family during the season and a business in the off-season.

What happens to families over time, and to teams, and to businesses, is that the power alignments shift, and then the tires no longer balance, and the vehicle can no longer be kept on the road. A newborn baby is happy being powerless, being cared for by parents who make all of the decisions and have all of the power. An 18-year-old is not. A six-year-old boy happily accepts the traditional values that his parents want him to accept; a 16-year-old girl wants to look forward and choose the values that seem right to her. When the power alignments shift the wheels are out of balance, and the family has reached the end of its run.

You will think in parts of this that I am writing about the Red Sox, but I am writing as much about the conservative father and the liberal mother, and I am writing as much about the conservative company president and the Left-leaning factory worker. There are a lot of things going on. My oldest daughter was married two weeks ago; my youngest son is 18 years old and in his last year of high school. My other son is between these two points, rather closer to the first. We are still family, but we are not the family that we were a couple of years ago; we are becoming a different family now. We have to start over and re-balance the wheels.

When a sports team has been together for a number of years, it becomes inevitable that the power alignments on the team will change. When a manager has been with a team for a number of years and has been highly successful, it is almost inevitable that he will become a power center in the organization. When you have veteran players who have been with the team for years and years they become power centers; when you have a General Manager who has been in his position for the better part of a decade and has been successful his power grows relative to his co-workers. This is not *wrong*, any more than it is wrong for a cooing baby to become a young woman, or wrong for her to pass through the role of a headstrong teenager along the way.

But when the power centers shift so substantially over a period of years, it is as if the four wheels of the vehicle were four different sizes, and it becomes impossible to keep the vehicle on the road. You have a car wreck; in our case, a high-speed car wreck. We have to start over and re-balance the wheels.

We come, now, to the real subject of our piece, which is the chaos on Wall Street. (This article was originally published at the height of the Occupy Wall Street movement, in 2011.) In a company as opposed to a team or a family there is more tolerance for selfishness and individual interests, and yet it is still true that the successful company must express and defend in its every action the interests of the group, rather than the interests of the individual. There is no "I" in "Company", either; how come nobody ever mentions that?

I have a good deal of sympathy for the Tea Partiers; I think they have valid points to make, and I support their efforts up to a point. But I also have at least as much sympathy for the Wall Street protestors, and I am in sympathy with their goals to at least the same extent. Their "goal" being what? To denounce greed.

A company can accommodate selfishness and greed on the part of its employees, up to a certain point. Within the last generation we have entirely lost track of the second half of that concept, the "up to a certain point" part. We have convinced ourselves that it is fine to pay top-level executives hundreds of times as much money as we pay the rank and file workers. It is *not* fine; it is destructive. It destroys companies, it damages the economy, and it damages society.

If you put a 62-inch tire on the passenger's side rear wheel, what would happen to your Mazda? Paying an executive a $20 million salary has the same effect on a company as putting a 62-inch tire on a passenger car. From that point on, you're never going to be able to drive the damn thing where you want it to go.

So far I have been speaking in analogies, and probably I have reached the limit of the analogy. Let's talk specifics. When the top executive is paid a very large salary, that immediately changes the culture of that organization. From that point on, everyone in the organization is looking to get as much *out* of the company as he can. It is virtually impossible to run a successful organization in which everyone is constantly trying to get as much *from* the company as he can. The company, from that point on, is in a kind of slow-burning civil war.

Every business that has chosen to pay its CEO a salary of tens of millions of dollars is on a course toward bankruptcy from that point forward. A company works only as long as those on all sides recognize their common interest in the success of the group. If the worker in the factory...well, why should we assume that the worker is in the factory? The worker may be in a factory, at a computer, in a sweatshop, on the asphalt or in the pit of a mine, or she could be in a thousand other places. If the worker and the executive both realize that their paycheck is dependent on doing something that neither of them can do alone, the company is in good shape.

Recognizing, of course, the dangers of submitting a two-paragraph history of labor relations...here they are:

In 19th century America, *owners* of companies routinely absorbed as profit a very large share of the income generated by the company as a whole. This led to widespread hatred of the rich, which divided America into rich and poor to the extent that the real threat of revolution hovered over the nation. Americans of the Teddy Roosevelt/Woodrow Wilson era recognized both the danger and the injustice of this. Their response was to give legal power to the Unions such that the Unions could successfully fight for a larger share of the income of companies.

There followed a long period of the democratization of wealth. Different people have different understandings of why this happened, but no one argues that it did not happen. Comparing America in 1980 to America in 1910, there was much more of an even division of wealth at the end of that era than at the beginning. It is the view of this author that the democratization of wealth in the years 1910 to 1980 was substantially to the credit of the Unions.

What no one quite anticipated was that the democratization of wealth would lead to the democratization of ownership, and that the democratization of ownership would lead to the "ownership" of companies becoming essentially anonymous. By 1980 millions of Americans were invested in the stock market directly or indirectly, and, as such, millions of Americans were the owners of most large businesses, through union and individual pension plans. *Who owns America's oil companies? You do.* It's true—and that became the next problem. We own the banks, we own the oil companies, we own the merchants.

In 19th century America, when large companies were owned by fantastically wealthy individuals, those individuals were often greedy and irresponsible until the end of their lives, when they gave all their money away and became beloved philanthropists, but this also put limits on executive compensation. The Robber Barons weren't going to pay outlandish executive compensation, because they didn't have to and they wanted the money for themselves. This kept the executives and the workers more or less on the same page: they were all fighting with the owners.

It has been observed by Malcolm Gladwell and others that, as recently as 1980, the salaries of executives were generally on the same scale as the salaries of workers. A company president earned *more* money than a factory worker, certainly, but more commonly three to five times as much, rather than three to five *hundred* times as much (or even, in some cases, three to five *thousand*). It is still true today in Japan and in many other countries that executive compensation is on the same scale as worker's compensation.

In America in the last generation, it has become the practice to compensate a small percentage of executives on an entirely different scale than workers, and even an entirely different scale than most executives. Gladwell has pointed to the role that baseball played in creating this expectation. In 1960 star baseball players were paid more than factory workers, but on a similar and overlapping scale. When sports stars and movie stars came to be paid hundreds of times as much as ordinary workers, star executives saw this as a justification to push for higher salaries of their own. Executive salaries began to rocket upward from that point.

It is my view that Gladwell is correct on that issue. But what I would point out as well is that, in the 19th century corporate ownership model, executives who pushed for spectacular salaries would—with exceptions, of course—have been thrown off the boat and told to swim for shore. By 1980 the democratization of wealth had created anonymous ownership structures. The Boards of Directors, in theory, represented the pension plans and stock portfolios that owned the companies, but the fact was: it wasn't their money. When the Executive Stars began to push for star salaries, the Boards of Directors should have pushed back, but...it wasn't their money. It understates the problem to say that they had little incentive to reign in executive compensation. The fact is that they had every incentive to feed the fire. As executive compensation exploded, salaries of Boards of Directors exploded.

The theory was that the Board of Directors represented ownership. The reality was that the Board of Directors became the highest rung of the executive ladder.

Among the things that America has done really, really well that makes us *America* is to institutionalize the concept of civilian control over the military. One of the things that we have failed to do, that makes us a weaker country than we should be, is to fail to generalize this concept. We don't let Generals decide when to go to war, but we *do* let retired teachers sit on school boards, we let lawyers run the justice system, and we let executives graduate to the Board of Directors. We would be better off if we would realize that, for the same reason that you don't let Generals decide what is in the best interests of the army, you don't let educators decide what is in the best interests of schools, you don't let lawyers run the justice system, and you don't let executives sit on the Board of Directors.

And you don't let athletes run baseball teams. Interestingly enough, we *do* recognize this principle now, about baseball. A generation ago, when I started writing about baseball, many General Managers or most General Managers were ex-players. When the salaries exploded, the owners of teams realized pretty quickly that, while many ex-players are extremely intelligent people, the experience of being a player did not provide the athlete with the ideal perspective on the problems of a General Manager. This happened in part because sports have clung to a 19th-century ownership model, in which the teams (except the Packers) are still owned by wealthy individuals, rather than by an anonymous collection of share-holders.

But getting back to the Wall Street banks and the other companies that are now run by thieves, pardon me, by high-salaried executives. The Boards of Directors were the firewall between Executive Stars, who were asking for and receiving constantly escalating compensation, and owners, who (by 1980) were in many cases faceless groups of hundreds of thousands of stock-holders.

Ah, you will argue; but if an executive is *worth* $5 million to the company, why should he not be paid $5 million? You may not argue this, but I watch Fox News. I like Fox News; they do a great job of representing their point of view. I only wish that someone would speak for the Left with the same clarity.

Please understand that when I say, "'you've got to be an idiot to believe," I don't *really* mean that you have to be an idiot to believe something. Very intelligent people believe all kinds of stupid stuff, because the world is simply so complicated that our ability to understand all the nuances of complex real-life problems is very limited.

Fox News would argue that if an executive is *worth* $5 million to his company, he should be paid $5 million. You've got to be an idiot to believe that any of these executives is really *worth* $5 million a year. These people don't get paid millions of dollars a year because they actually earn millions of dollars a year for their companies; they get paid millions of dollars a year because they occupy a strong position in the political power struggles over the money generated by the company as a whole.

Look, here's what I think happens; I don't claim to be able to prove any of this. Relate it to a baseball. Suppose that the agent for a baseball player—Porky McBling of the Blue Knights—picked through his RBIs for the season and said, "Look here. The game on July 6 was 4-3, the Knights team behind. Porky hit a two-run double and they won that game. Porky won that game for them. Here's another one; game was 4-2, Porky hit a three-run homer, the Blue Knights won, 5-4. Porky won that game for them.

"Altogether, Porky drove in 76 runs for the Blue Knights, which led directly to 23 victories for them, or 28% of the team's 82 victories. The Blue Knights payroll was $106 million. 28% of that would be $30 million, but Porky isn't asking to be paid $30 million. Porky only wants $12 million. This is a very fair salary given his contribution to the team."

Because we have sophisticated tools to analyze baseball and are in the habit of using them, we are able to see through that argument very easily. Porky was able to drive in two runs in the July 6 game only because two runners had reached base ahead of him, and these two runs won the game for the Blue Knights only because three runs had been scored earlier, and these five runs were enough only because of the performance of the pitchers and the fielders.

But businesses rarely or never have equally sophisticated tools to evaluate the contributions of each employee. The executive says "I opened up the Chilean market for us by establishing contact for us with the Chilean WalMart. Our sales in Chile last year were $213 million, leading to a profit of $41 million on our operations in Chile. I deserve to be compensated for that. $10 million is nothing compared to the contributions I have made to this company." Yes, you opened up the Chilean market for us—but only because somebody else built the products that you convinced them to buy, and only because some engineer or inventor designed those products, and these products sold $213 million, but only because somebody in the warehouse filled every order, and somebody else put every widget in a box, and somebody else loaded that box on a truck, and somebody else drove that truck to the airport.

The explosion of executive salaries is really about the *failure* of ownership, about the weakness and exploitation of ownership by a coalition of those they employ to run their companies. Returning to the four-tires analogy, modern ownership (in most areas, not in baseball) is a flat tire. I am in danger here of using "Conservative" as a synonym for "selfishness," which is not my intention, for the Conservative believes not in selfishness or greed; rather, the Conservative believes that the selfishness and greed which are integral parts of human nature provide the coiled energy that drives society forward. This is more realistic than believing that that energy can be replaced by altruism, which is not to speak ill, either, of altruism.

In any case, the Conservative advocates for respect for value, arguing that the lack of respect for value deprives society of its creative energy. I have no problem with this argument. My argument is that I simply do not believe that those bankers and executives who are paid multi-million dollar salaries have actually earned them. I do not believe that this is their actual value. I believe that they are paid salaries greatly exceeding their actual value because they have the political power within their companies to demand such salaries, and those who should resist paying them, on behalf of the owners, have no real incentive to do so.

For that matter, I don't believe that $20 million baseball players are worth $20 million, either, but that's a different argument. In any case, we have a situation in which some people are being paid very large salaries while others are not doing well. What do we do about it?

Here we have a divide between the organized and the disorganized Left. Political commentators have made much of the political divide between the Country Club Republicans and the Tea Partiers—the organized Right and the disorganized Right—but the same divide exists on the Left. The organized Left wants

a) To tax the millionaires and billionaires, and
b) To strengthen the Unions.

The disorganized Left wants Wall Street to stop paying these ridiculous salaries.

President Obama's argument to tax the millionaires and billionaires is falling on deaf ears because it comes across as a denial that government is spending too much money. The Tea Partiers argue—and I agree with them—that government is trying to do too many things, that government is trying to do things that it is incapable of doing well, and that, because government is trying to do too many things and is trying to do things that it is incapable of doing well, it is just spending too much money. When the President responds to that argument with "tax the millionaires and billionaires," it comes across as an attempt to deny that government is spending too much money. "We're *not* spending too much money," Obama seems to be saying. "We just have to increase taxes on the millionaires and billionaires." Until President Obama admits that government is too large and is spending too much money, his pleas for additional tax revenue are going nowhere. Once he admits that government is way too large and is spending way too much money—not admits this once off-handedly, but acknowledges it as a fundamental truth, acknowledges it repeatedly and adopts some sort of program to address the problem—then I, for one, will be with him in saying, "Let's increase taxes on the rich until we get the deficit under control." Until he does that, I'm with the Tea Partiers.

If one wishes to see a more equitable distribution of wealth—which I do—taxing the rich is in any case a limited strategy because of the ability of the rich to evade taxable events. Raising taxes on the rich funnels as much money to tax lawyers as it does to government. There is an element of the Left that remains under the spell of a delusion that the Unions can still be what the Unions were a hundred years ago, that they can still play that very valuable role that Unions once played in getting a more equitable distribution of wealth. It seems clear that they can't, for two reasons. First, the Unions were given, in the Teddy Roosevelt era, legal powers with which they could do battle with owners. This is not fundamentally a battle between ownership and workers; it is fundamentally a battle between workers and Executive Stars. Owners are as much a victim of executive greed as are workers. The tools that the Unions were given are ill-equipped for the modern multi-national struggle, and Unions are ill-equipped for a battle in which they and the owners of companies should be on the same side. Second, the American people no longer are with the Unions and no longer believe in Unions. The Unions have forfeited the moral high ground by a century of greedy, unrealistic and selfish behavior which, while no worse than the behavior of owners or executives, causes them to be seen as no better.

The organized Left, then, is unrealistic (the pro-Union crowd) and in denial about the nature of their problem (the tax-the-rich crowd.) What are we left with?

We are left to condemn greed. It is useful to condemn greed; it is appropriate to condemn greed, and it is, to an extent, satisfying to condemn greed. The Wall Street protestors are condemning greed in a manner that is clumsy, inarticulate, ill-mannered, unfocused and misdirected. They are not making an economic point or in any case not a cogent economic point; they are making a moral point: greed is destructive; greed is corrosive. I don't disagree. Self-interest is the coiled spring that drives sports teams and great businesses, but greed destroys companies in the same way that selfishness destroys baseball and football and basketball teams and leagues. There is no easy way to recognize when self-interest passes into greed, but wherever that point was, the Executive Stars of Wall Street rolled past it several years ago.

———·———

The 300-Win Pool

by Bill James

———·—

Early Wynn in 1963, asked if he was disappointed that Warren Spahn had beaten him to 300 wins, said that no, he was delighted, because this way he (Wynn) would always be the last pitcher to win 300 games. Nobody would ever win 300 games again.

In the late 1970s I tried to publish an article entitled "300 Game Winners: There is going to be a flood," the premise of the article being that we were positioned to see a whole bunch of pitchers win 300 games in the 1980s—Carlton, Seaver, Gaylord Perry, Sutton, Niekro, Nolan Ryan. The editor thought I was nuts. It was obvious that this was going to happen, if you looked at their ages and win totals, but the editor wouldn't believe it. After those guys there was another round of sportswriters claiming that Nolan Ryan would be the last-ever 300-game winner, and then there was another round of them—Clemens, Maddux, Johnson, Glavine. People for some reason want to believe that 300-game winners are going extinct and will rush to that conclusion at any opportunity.

There are certain factors operating over time to make 300-game winners less common, and there are certain factors operating to make them more common. My analysis of these various factors would be no better than yours, and, honestly, I'm not sure that anything relevant to this issue has changed in the last 25 years, except perhaps for the expansions of the 1990s creating a few more 300-win candidates. The other things that changed—the DH Rule, the change from the 4-man to the 5-man rotation, the lengthening of the schedule to 162 games—all happened more than 25 years ago, and several pitchers have already won 300 games entirely after all of those changes, clearly establishing that it is still possible for a pitcher to win 300 games.

145

The bullpens? Well...but starting pitchers get about as many decisions (per team) now as they did 25 years ago. In 1987 starting pitchers accounted for 115 decisions per team; the bullpens, for 47. In 2012 starting pitchers accounted for 117 per team; the bullpens, 45. There has been no shift of *decisions* to the bullpen in the last 25 years; thus, nothing has happened there that seems relevant to a pitcher's chance of winning 300 games.

That is all old business. I had a new thought here, which was that we could easily measure the *pool* of potential 300-game winners. What I have done before is to estimate a given pitcher's chance of winning 300 games. What is James Shields' chance of winning 300 games? What is CC Sabathia's chance? What I realized we could do, thinking about this now, is to measure the *pool* of candidates—comparing not CC Sabathia to James Shields, but 2013 to 1974.

First, we set up a very simple set of rules to assess the strength of each 300-win candidate. The rules are:

1) The pitcher gets one point for each 20 wins that he has in his career.
2) The pitcher gets one point for each 3 years that he is younger than 45 years of age.
3) Points awarded under rules one and two are discounted by 20% per year if the pitcher pitched less than 200 innings, 40% if less than 150 innings, 60% if less than 100 innings, and 80% if less than 50 innings.

And there's a fourth rule that we'll get to in a minute. The highest-scoring pitchers of all time are two 19th-century pitchers and Christy Mathewson after the 1911 season; they all score at "19". Mathewson after the 1911 season had 289 wins, which is 14 points, and he was 30 years old, so he gets 5 points for that. That's a total of 19. All of the (three) pitchers who score at 19 did in fact go on to win 300 games.

A bunch of pitchers score at 18, but the last one of those was Walter Johnson in 1919, so that's not too relevant to today. A bunch of pitchers score at 17, but the last one of those was Grover Cleveland Alexander in 1923. Greg Maddux after the 2003 season and Roger Clemens after the 2001 season scored at 16. Mike Mussina, Randy Johnson, and Tom Glavine got to 15, as well as Clemens and Maddux.

The fourth rule is that if a pitcher has more than 280 career wins, his score cannot be less than his career win total, minus 280, regardless of age or innings pitched. I said there were three pitchers at "19", but actually there was a fourth. Early Wynn after the 1962 season had 299 career wins, so he also was at "19".

Historically, four pitchers have scored at "19", and all four did go on to 300 wins. In terms of exact numbers, 9 of 11 have reached 300 who have been at 18 (82%), 10 of 12 who have been at 17 (83%), 20 of 36 who have been at 16 (56%), 26 of 51 from 15 (51%), 35 of 90 from 14 (39%), 32 of 143 from 13 (22%), 40 of 247 from 12 (16%), and 38 of 373 from 11 (10%). 5% of pitchers who have been at "10" have gone on to win 300 games, 3% of pitchers from "9", 1% of pitchers from "8", and 2/10ths of one percent from "7".

It is essentially consistent with the record, then, to value a pitcher at 19 at "90", 18 at "80", 17 at "70"...on down to 11 at "10". That's a simple image of the "pool value" of a pitcher at each level. We will assign a pitcher at 10 a pool value of 5, a pitcher at 9 a pool value of 3, and a pitcher at 8 a pool value of 1. Pitchers at 7 or less we will just ignore, since they haven't shown us anything that suggests they will be 300-game winners.

In this way we can measure the pool of potential 300-game winners after each season in major league history. After the first season of major league baseball there were 8 pitchers who qualified for the pool, but their total pool value was just 14...obviously, nobody could establish himself as a serious 300-win candidate in just one season. These numbers went up quickly in the first few years

Year	Candidates	Total Pool
1876	8	14
1877	4	19
1878	6	33
1879	9	69

And continued to ascend rapidly through the 1880s:

Year	Candidates	Total Pool
1880	10	117
1881	11	86
1882	21	147
1883	26	245
1884	39	442
1885	32	386
1886	40	486
1887	41	606
1888	44	560
1889	45	610

A pool value of 610 indicates, in general terms, that there should be about six active pitchers who will get to 300 career wins—not counting any active pitcher who already has 300 career wins;

those are not 300-win "candidates", so we ignore them. In fact, only four of the 1889 pitchers did go on to 300 wins (Mickey Welch, John Clarkson, Tim Keefe and Old Hoss Radbourne), so they under-achieved a little bit, as a group.

Pitchers from the 1880s often were credited with 40 wins a year, sometimes 50, so it didn't take a pitcher 20 years to get to 300 wins. The pitching business changed substantially in 1893, when the pitcher's mound was moved back to 60 feet, 6 inches. Keefe and Welch won their 300th games in 1890, which made them no longer 300-win candidates, so that immediately shrank the pool, and then the game changed in the mid-1890s.

I suppose I should dwell on that a moment, make sure people are keeping up. In 1876 most teams used one starting pitcher every game. The pitching distance was shorter, and pitchers threw under-handed, delivering the ball at the height requested by the hitter; the pitcher was more the initiator of the action than the determiner of the outcome. These things changed quickly. By the mid-1880s most teams used two starting pitchers; by the early 1890s, three. By 1900 some teams were using four-man starting rotations.

However, the conditions of the game, which involved many double-headers and frequent rainouts and longer breaks for travel, did not allow for great regularity in pitcher usage patterns. Even though a team might have a four-man pitching "rotation", they also might have a five-game, three-day series or a four-day, seven-game series, so pitchers would start on short rest or long rest with no great predictability. Up until 1920, teams would sometimes start a pitcher Friday and again on Sunday in a big series—or if a starting pitcher pitched poorly, he might disappear from the rotation for ten days without any explanation. It was a rotation/catch-as-catch can.

Anyway, the 300-win candidates pool went down in 1890 be-cause two of the leading candidates crossed the wire at 300 wins, whereas the number of possible candidates went up because there was a third league in 1890. The "610" pool of 300-win candidates in 1889 is the largest the pool has ever been. We've never gotten back to 610:

Year	Candidates	Total Pool
1890	58	544
1891	46	475
1892	35	405
1893	33	398
1894	37	419
1895	32	409
1896	30	320
1897	33	371
1898	40	472
1899	36	372

Through the 1890s, 30-win seasons were commonplace, so 300 wins was only ten years' work. Thirty-seven pitchers won thirty games in the 1890s, as opposed to ten from 1900-1909, seven from 1910-1919, and four since 1920. A pitcher could get to be a serious 300-win candidate pretty quickly. The pool of *potential* 300-game winners shrank next when Kid Nichols (1899) and Cy Young (1901) crossed the 300-win threshold, then recovered as Christy Mathewson, Eddie Plank and others emerged as serious 300-win candidates, the "others" being a series of guys who didn't make it—Addie Joss, Ed Walsh, Rube Walberg, Iron Man McGinnity, Jack Powell, Vic Willis, etc:

Year	Candidates	Total Pool
1900	26	226
1901	42	126
1902	44	168
1903	40	200
1904	53	228
1905	52	281
1906	59	364
1907	51	382
1908	45	364
1909	44	360

After 1910 the dominant pitchers in the game were Walter Johnson and Pete Alexander. Christy Mathewson crossed the 300-win mark in 1912. After that the pool of 300-win candidates stayed in the range of 200 to 300 points—two to three likely 300-game winners—for the rest of the decade, with Pete and Walter being the biggest part of that:

Year	Candidates	Total Pool
1910	47	362
1911	49	409
1912	42	274
1913	44	204
1914	65	293
1915	73	283
1916	49	211
1917	54	267
1918	38	207
1919	41	265

The numbers hung in that range for about ten more years, and then dropped sharply in the early 1930s:

Year	Candidates	Total Pool
1920	51	246
1921	44	216
1922	39	257
1923	45	320
1924	45	246
1925	40	309
1926	38	257
1927	41	220
1928	36	217
1929	43	236
1930	42	177
1931	48	180
1932	50	174
1933	43	149

There was a dramatic "aging" of the major league population in the late 1920s, which I think was driven by economics. The popularity of baseball exploded after 1920 due to

1) Babe Ruth, and

2) Throwing the gamblers out the window.

I *think* what happened was that, as attendance went up, salaries went up; and as salaries went up, there was a strong incentive for major league players to stay in the game rather than to retire. In any case there were many, many more older players in the majors in the late 1920s than ten years earlier. When those players finally gave up the ghost, there was a youth movement in the 1930 era, and in that era there were increasing *numbers* of 300-win candidates, but most of them were young pitchers who were a long way from 300 wins.

The only pitcher to win 300 games between Pete Alexander (early 1920s) and Spahn and Wynn (early 1960s) was Lefty Grove. Red Ruffing and Bob Feller might have gotten there had it not been for World War II; in fact, I think we should say of each of them that they *probably* would have made it to 300 had it not been for World War II.

Anyway, something very interesting happened to the pool of 300-win candidates in the mid-1930s:

Year	Candidates	Total Pool
1933	43	149
1934	47	151
1935	36	240
1936	39	240
1937	35	223
1938	31	184
1939	35	147
1940	31	230
1941	31	152
1942	31	121
1943	27	52
1944	29	76
1945	26	91
1946	17	67

Between 1934 and 1935, the number of candidates for 300 wins dropped from 47 to 36—but the size of the pool increased from 151 to 240. What happened?

In a sense this is a normal maturation process. You have a group of young pitchers; they all look great, and any one of them has a chance to win 300 games, but only a slim chance. Over time, most of them fall off the radar, while one or two step forward to be serious 300-win candidates. It just happened that in 1934-1935 this happened in an accelerated time frame. In 1934 Lefty Grove had an injury season, and his run appeared to be over. This left the top 300-win candidates in the game as Ted Lyons (score of 12), Guy Bush (11), Fat Freddie Fitzsimmons (11), and Earl Whitehill (11). In 1935 Grove won 20 games, re-establishing himself as a serious contender, while his teammate Wes Ferrell, also injured in 1933 and 1934, won 25, putting him in a strong position as well; after the 1935 season he was 27 years old and had 141 career wins with five 20-win seasons.

After the 1935 season the leading 300-win candidates were Grove (14), Ferrell (13), Bush (12), Whitehill (12), while five new pitchers had stepped up to 11.

During the War the number of 300-win candidates in the game fell to historic lows, while 1946 was a "starting-over" season, almost like 1876. After 1946 the number of 300-win candidates began to grow steadily:

Year	Candidates	Total Pool
1946	17	67
1947	25	94
1948	26	106
1949	37	119
1950	36	149
1951	30	113
1952	29	101
1953	28	114
1954	33	134
1955	28	146
1956	32	198
1957	33	185
1958	28	188
1959	38	257
1960	37	255

In the 1950s there were three obvious candidates for 300 career wins: Warren Spahn, Early Wynn, and Robin Roberts. Roberts was actually the best 300-win candidate, among the three of them, for most of his career. Roberts won his 200th game at age 31, whereas Wynn and Spahn didn't win their 200th games until they were 35. But Roberts was worked very, very hard by a series of bad Philadelphia teams in the late 1950s, had some difficult years, and fell short of 300, whereas Spahn and Wynn held on to reach the target.

Spahn crossed 300 wins in 1961, Wynn in 1963, but the 300-win pool hardly noticed, as expansion, a longer schedule, and a pitcher-friendly environment created a pool of 300-win candidates behind them—Koufax, Gibson, Marichal, Drysdale, etc. None of those guys made it, but in the mid-1960s, they were all good candidates:

Year	Candidates	Total Pool
1960	37	255
1961	38	121
1962	40	237
1963	46	215
1964	40	252
1965	46	259
1966	45	204
1967	47	202
1968	58	250
1969	61	235

What followed, emerging about 1970, was the most remarkable group of starting pitchers in the history of baseball. I mentioned before the ones who won 300 games—Carlton, Seaver, Niekro, Perry, Nolan Ryan, Sutton—but the list of outstanding pitchers in that generation who *didn't* get to 300 wins is even longer: Ferguson Jenkins, Tommy John, Luis Tiant, Blyleven, Jim Palmer, Catfish Hunter, Vida Blue, Jim Kaat, Mickey Lolich.

The mind searches endlessly for the causes of every effect, and it will never come up empty. It may come up with the *wrong* answer, but it will always come up with an answer; this is just how we are wired. What I note about this generation of pitchers is how many of them were born *during* World War II or else very early in the Baby Boom era. Carlton and Seaver were born in 1944, Ferguson Jenkins in late 1943, Sutton in early 1945. Denny McLain was born in '44, Jim Palmer in '45. I always think that these guys had an edge in their youth because, competing with the Baby Boomers as kids in the less-organized play of that era, they were always the big kids, the kids who were a year older than the guys they were playing against. Maybe it's an arbitrary explanation.

In any case, in the 1970s there was a remarkable explosion of pitchers who pitched very large numbers of innings every year, with great effectiveness, and did it for a long time. Catfish Hunter got into the Hall of Fame for a simple reason: he retired in time to get to the ballot first. Catfish Hunter was seven and a half years younger than Jim Kaat—but retired four years before Kaat did. When Catfish hit the ballot in the mid-1980s he was the best pitcher on the ballot. By the time Kaat got there, the ballot had been invaded by 300-game winners and near-300 game winners like Ferguson Jenkins and Jim Palmer. Kaat was pushed way back in the line. Jack Morris was a very, very good pitcher who had a wonderful career—but if had come up ten years earlier, he would have been just another one of those guys, another one of that long list of magnificent starting pitchers from that era. I won't even mention Jerry Koosman and Jerry Reuss and Rick Reuschel—but in another generation, they'd be near the top of the list. It was an amazing time.

This abundance of starting pitchers is reflected in the growth of the 300-win pool in those years:

Year	Candidates	Total Pool
1970	56	239
1971	66	350
1972	58	330
1973	67	396
1974	67	435
1975	64	455
1976	64	473
1977	63	374
1978	63	478
1979	58	452
1980	67	481

In 1967 the 300-win pool was 202 points—likely about two 300-game winners. There were actually at least six 300-game winners active at that time, but in 1967 we had no way of suspecting that. By 1980 the 300-win pool had expanded to 481 points—the largest it has been since 1890. For 1981 we get a bad read on the data because of the strike, and after 1981 the pool begins to shrink as pitchers began to roll past 300 wins.

Year	Candidates	Total Pool
1980	67	481
1981	20	118
1982	57	430
1983	60	335
1984	61	331
1985	61	282
1986	59	206
1987	54	257
1988	58	294
1989	57	275

As there are remarkably many #1 starters in the 1970s, there are remarkably few in the 1980s. Most of the 1980s data is accounted for, actually, by holdovers from the 1970s. The top four pitchers on the list from 1985 are Sutton, Ryan, Blyleven and Jerry Reuss. Even in 1988 the top two names on the list are Blyleven and Nolan Ryan.

Gradually, another generation of star pitchers began to emerge. By 1990 Roger Clemens, Greg Maddux, Randy Johnson and Tom Glavine were in the majors and in the rotation, as well as worthy candidates like David Cone, Bret Saberhagen, Dwight Gooden, Frank Viola and Fernando Valenzuela. The pool from the 1990s was not small; it merely looked small compared to the lake from the 1970s. It was in this generation, the early 1990s, that it once more became fashionable to say that there would never be another 300-game winner. By 2001 the fallacy of this had become apparent:

Year	Candidates	Total Pool
1990	49	206
1991	54	218
1992	61	252
1993	65	254
1994	24	46
1995	36	105
1996	53	181
1997	52	203
1998	57	235
1999	52	233
2000	43	257
2001	43	281

And where are we now? Well, the pool of 300-win candidates is thinner than it has been since the mid-1950s, discounting the "bad data reads" from the strike seasons. This is the data since 2000:

Year	Candidates	Total Pool
2000	43	257
2001	43	281
2002	49	257
2003	52	219
2004	47	224
2005	55	277
2006	54	252
2007	42	153
2008	52	249
2009	49	136
2010	53	189
2011	50	190
2012	49	153
2013	40	142

The leading candidates among current pitchers include (or included, at the end of the 2012 season) Roy Halladay, Verlander and Greinke, all of whom have had some setbacks.

Are 300-game winners dead? 300 game winners would be dead if the pool size was 18, or 20, or zero. 142...that still means there are probably one or two now-active pitchers who will get to 300 wins. As I see it, nothing really has changed, in regard to winning 300 games, since the transition from four-man to five-man rotations was completed by the late 1980s. But the 300-win pool *is*, in fact, smaller than it has been since I became a baseball fan.

THE ZANESVILLE ANIMAL MASSACRE

by Bill James

———·——

In re the weird story out of Zanesville...you ever been to Zanesville, by the way? It's worth going for the churches. I don't know if they had a church-building war there or what, but Zanesville has the most impressive collection of old churches you'll ever see in a town that size in America—or a town twice that size or three times that size.

Anyway, in re the guy who killed himself and turned loose a private zoo, leading to the deaths of 18 Bengal tigers, or, as the media insists on saying, 18 "rare" Bengal tigers...obviously *something* happened here that should never happen; I'm not arguing that point. Obviously people who keep tigers in three-room apartments have a screw loose; not arguing that, either. We can't be killing tigers en masse, nor have them roaming the countryside. We can't *risk* things like that happening; we need some sort of societal safeguards against that.

But the news coverage of this fairly horrific event, in my view, was slanted in a very unproductive direction, featuring

a) every story they could find about some snake that got out of its cage in the middle of the night and killed a baby, etc., and
b) interviews with self-righteous people who were trying to create the impression that the housing of wild animals with American families is out of control.

CNN reported with alarm that "there are now more Bengal tigers in private hands in America than there are living in the wild."

If there are more Bengal tigers living in America than in the wild, that's a bad thing? That's not a bad thing; it's a good thing.

157

It's a bad thing that they're almost extinct in the wild; it's a good thing that at least we are keeping the species going in a makeshift manner. What would be better is if there were three times as many as there are. What would be better is if there were also more jaguars, cheetahs, ocelots, kangaroos, Hawaiian monk seals and howler monkeys squirreled away here and there—enough to permanently protect the species.

Look, everybody wishes that we could protect the natural habitat for these species, and we will—eventually. Eventually, two or three hundred years down the road, we'll succeed in having areas set aside around the globe where animals are safe. But until we get there, the more of these animals we have in private hands, the better.

My wife makes 99% of the rules in our house, but one rule I insisted on, when the kids were small, is that I wasn't going to have "pets" in the house that aren't really pets. Fish, birds, cats, dogs… that's fine. No spiders, ferrets, snakes, gerbils, hamsters; if you would kill the thing if it came into the house on its own, that's not a pet.

But that's me; that's a rule for my house. It seems to me that people are arguing that because I wouldn't do it, *nobody* should do it. Because *I* wouldn't want to keep a crocodile, *nobody* should be keeping crocodiles.

And occasionally somebody gets killed; that's terrible, everything possible should be done to prevent that. But 40 people are killed every year in skateboarding accidents, and we don't ban skateboards. God knows how many people are killed in car races, and we don't ban car racing. Dozens of people are killed every year in propane tank accidents; we haven't banned propane.

If you want to make a rule that people who keep tigers have to have some reasonable amount of *space* for the tiger to live, some place outside with sunshine and moving water…that's fine; I can support that. If you want to propose rules to ensure that we don't have another Zanesville…sure. Even if you want to require these people to register with the city and have the city come out and inspect the property, that's OK.

But if you're just concerned about the fact that these animals are in *private* hands and that people are interacting with them in ways that *you and I* wouldn't choose to do…Mind Your Own Business. The more we can do to establish a private trade in rare and exotic animals, the more rare and exotic animals will survive until the efforts to create safe zones for them reach maturity.

Tough Stretches and Soft Patches

by Bill James

On July 30, 1954, the Chicago White Sox White Sox played a four-game series against the Philadelphia A's. The A's were not a good team; they lost 103 games that year (51-103), and July was their worst month (7-23). After the four games against the A's, the White Sox played four games against the Red Sox (69-85 in 1954), and then three games against the Senators (66-88). After the Senators the White Sox played two games against the Baltimore Orioles (54-100), and four against the Tigers (68-86), and then four more against the Orioles (54-100). And here's the kicker: of those 21 games, the first 17 games were at home.

In that stretch of 21 games the White Sox went 17-4, outscored their opponents 96-54 and had a 2.47 ERA from their starting pitchers. In the 60 years of data that I have to study, that is the "softest" part of a schedule that any team has ever had.

One of the teams in 2013 in the Eastern Division of the American League had a ridiculously soft part of their schedule, during which they were kicking Astros and taking names, so I got interested in identifying the softest (and toughest) stretches of games that any team has played. The first thing I had to do, of course, was to create a method to study the issue.

Here's the method. First, I figured for each team their won-lost record in their last 100 games, and in their last 62 games. Last year's games count; if your team went 57-105 last year, odds are you are not in first place this year, either. I added the 100-game and 62-game records together to form a 162-game won-lost record for each team, and figured winning percentages. Then I grouped teams in this way:

A .570 or better won-lost record (93-69 or better) is a Level 4 opponent, or a "post season quality" opponent,

A .500 to .56999 won-lost record (81-81 to 92-70) is a Level 3 opponent, or a ".500+" opponent,

A .430 to .49999 won-lost record (70-92 to 80-82) is a Level 2 opponent or a "sub-.500" opponent, and

A sub-.430 opponent (69-93 or worse) is a Level 1 opponent or a "weak" or "bad" opposition team.

To these 1-4 levels, I added 1 point if it was a road game, so that each game had a "toughness level" of 1 to 5, one being the softest opponent and 5 the toughest.

The 1954 White Sox had the softest stretch of 20 games. I was looking for 20-game stretches of games, although the White Sox run was actually 21 games. The American League in 1954 is peculiar, in that there are five pretty bad teams in an eight-team league. The Indians went 111-43 that year and the Yankees went 103-51, so the rest of the league was 110 games under .500. The Red Sox finished in the first division with a record of 69-85.

On the other side of the study, the toughest stretch of 20 games that any team ever had (in the last 60 years) was the Milwaukee Brewers in April of 1978. The Brewers in April of 1978 played exactly 20 games. They played the Orioles, the Yankees, the Orioles again, the Red Sox, the Yankees again, the Red Sox again, and the Royals. Those were the four best teams in the American League at that time, whether you use their 1977 records to tell you that or their 1978 records, and 13 of the 20 games were on the road. The starting pitchers the Brewers faced in the first 20 games of 1978 were Mike Flanagan, Dennis Martinez, Scott McGregor, Catfish Hunter, Ken Holtzman, Dennis Martinez again, Jim Palmer, Nelson Briles, Scott McGregor again, Mike Torrez, Dennis Eckersley, Bill Lee, Ed Figueroa, Dick Tidrow, Catfish Hunter again, Bill Lee again, Mike Torrez again, Steve Busby, Dennis Leonard and Rich Gale. For those of you younger than 50, those were good pitchers.

The Brewers had lost 95 games in 1977. In 1978, despite this challenging April schedule, they managed to go 9-11, which set the stage for a terrific season in which the Brewers won 93 games and emerged as the fourth powerhouse in the American League East.

Other teams have had extremely soft 20-game stretches. The Angels in May of 1966 had a 25-game stretch of games in which they played only the four worst teams in the American League (the Yankees, Red Sox, A's and Senators.) From April 30 through May 25 they played eight games against the Senators, seven against the Red Sox, five against the A's and five against the Yankees. They went just 13-12 in those 25 games, missing their chance to set themselves up for a better season.

In 1978, while the Brewers were playing all of the league's toughest teams, the A's (in the same time frame) were playing all of the league's worst teams—that is, all of them except themselves. The A's, who finished 69-93 in 1978, actually started the season 18-5. They started the season 18-5 in part because they played 23 straight games against teams that had finished under .500 in 1977 and would do so again in 1978. During those 23 games the A's starting pitchers had an ERA of 1.66. The world got even with them, though, in June of that year, when they had to play a stretch of 34 consecutive games against teams that each won 87 or more games that year (May 29 through July 2.) That A's team had one of the easiest and one of the toughest stretches of games of any team on record.

The Mariners from April 21 through May 31, 1979, played 37 consecutive games against teams that would finish the season with a winning record. Of course, I didn't mark games as "easy" or "tough" based on final-season won-lost records; I'm just using the final-season won-lost records as an easy reference point. 34 of the 37 games were marked "4" or "5". Their "easiest" series in that stretch was a series against the Red Sox. The Red Sox "recent won-lost record" coming into the series was 92-70, but 92-70 is Group 3, and the series was at home for the Mariners, so that's a "3". All of the other games were "4" or "5".

The Reds in 1966 opened the season playing a very difficult stretch of games, but there is a little-known effect here which is kind of skewing our data. As the season goes on, there is a tendency of the leagues to pull apart. .600 teams tend to play .630 baseball in September, whereas .400 teams tend to play .370 baseball. It doesn't color the stats a whole lot, but when you search for the MOST difficult or the MOST easy stretches of games, based on how the opposition has played in the last 100 games and the last 62 games, you tend to get a lot of April games, because the hottest and coldest stretches tend (to a very small degree) to be in September, and, when you look at a very large number of games, the extremes will tend to concentrate in the periods most favorable to extremes, even though you're dealing with a pretty small effect.

So when I looked for the toughest and softest parts of the schedule in the 21st century, I excluded stretches of games in April and May and looked only at stretches ending no earlier than June 1. Since 2000 the toughest stretch of games that any team has had was by the Oakland A's in 2009, a 21-game stretch from July 6 through July 30. Here again I'll give you their opponents end-of-season won-lost records, although that wasn't what I used to identify the toughest stretches: The A's in 2009 played the Red Sox (95-67), the Rays (84-78, but playing much better at that time), the Angels (97-65, Western Division champions), the Twins (87-76, Central Division Champions), the Yankees (103-59) and the Red Sox again. Fifteen of the 21 games were on the road, and they had to fly across the country twice.

That ties as the toughest stretch of games that any team has had in the 21st century with a string of games that the Blue Jays had in September of 2008. Actually beginning on August 16, the Jays played 28 consecutive games against the Red Sox (95-67), the Rays (97-65), the Yankees (89-73), the Twins (88-75) and the White Sox (89-74). 16 of the 28 games were on the road, and 15 of the 28 were against the Red Sox and the Rays (95-67 and 97-65).

As to the easiest stretches of games...the Yankees in 2002 didn't play anybody good after September 4th. From September 5 to the end of the season in 2002 (24 games) the Yankees played the Tigers (55-106), Orioles (67-95), White Sox, Devil Rays (55-106), Tigers (55-106), Devil Rays (55-106) and Orioles (67-95). The White Sox were 81-81, but not playing particularly well at that point of the schedule. The Yankees, eight and a half games ahead when they began that stretch of games, cruised into the post-season on auto-pilot.

The Red Sox had an almost equally soft schedule at the end of the 2001 season. The Red Sox' last series before the 9-11 attack on the World Trade Center was against the Yankees. They were off on Monday (9-10), and then on 9-11 they were supposed to play the Rays. That series was delayed for a week while the country struggled to get back on our feet, and then the Red Sox played the D Rays (62-99), Tigers (66-95), Orioles (63-98), and then the Tigers, Rays and Orioles again. The Red Sox failed to take advantage of the opportunity, however, going just 10-10 in those 20 games, and failing to qualify for the post-season.

———··———

EXPERIMENT IN SUMMARY

by Bill James

———·———

The History of Rome in 10 Words

A small city grew gradually to become a vast empire.

The History of Rome in 25 Words

Under kings and emperors and as a republic, Rome grew constantly for almost a thousand years, and became the greatest power of the ancient world.

The History of Rome in 50 Words

Founded 753 BC, Rome was ruled by kings until 509 BC, and was a republic then until Julius Caesar took power in 46 BC. After Caesar Rome became an empire, with an emperor. Rome's growth from a small city to a great empire was sustained by their success in wars.

The History of Rome in 100 Words

Founded about 753 BC, Rome was a belligerent little town that consistently prevailed in conflicts with rivals, and thus grew gradually in size and influence. Ruled by kings until 509 BC, Rome transitioned into a disciplined, well-organized republic which sustained excellence in military preparation and capacity, and thus continued to grow for hundreds of years. Ruled by an emperor from about 27 BC, Rome reached the zenith of its power in the years 100 to 180 AD, under the rulers known as the Five Good Emperors. A series of corrupt and incompetent rulers allowed Rome to slip gradually into history.

The History of Rome in 200 Words

Founded about 753 BC, Rome was a belligerent little town that consistently prevailed in conflicts with neighborhood cities, and thus grew gradually in size and influence. Ruled in its early years by elected kings, Rome fell gradually under the power of tyrants. The Roman nobility revolted in 509 BC, expelled the kings, and established a republic.

With a disciplined, educated noble class and a strong ethic of service, the Roman republic continued to grow and thrive. This led them eventually into conflict with the other great powers of the region, most notably the Carthaginians, with whom Rome fought a series of wars from roughly 264 BC until 146 BC. After those wars Rome was divided between its own nobility and reformers, and these fought a series of civil wars culminating in a disastrous conflict that brought Julius Caesar to power in 46 BC. After the death of Caesar, civil war brought to power Rome's greatest ruler, the Emperor Augustus.

As an empire, Rome reached the zenith of its power in the years 100 to 180 AD, under the rulers known as the Five Good Emperors. A series of corrupt and incompetent rulers allowed the Roman Empire to fracture and crumble.

The History of Rome in 500 Words

Founded about 753 BC, Rome was a belligerent little town that consistently prevailed in conflicts with neighborhood cities, and thus grew gradually in size and influence. Ruled in its early years by elected kings, often men of excellent judgment, Rome fell gradually under the power of tyrants. The Roman nobility revolted in 509 BC, after the son of King Tarquinius Superbas raped a noblewoman known for her virtue (Lucretia). The nobility expelled the kings, and established a republic.

For a generation after that the Roman city/state was often under attack, and sometimes on the verge of obliteration. But with a disciplined, educated nobility and a strong ethic of service, the Roman republic recovered, and by the end of the 5th century BC (400 BC) was once more growing constantly larger and more powerful. This led them into conflict with the other great powers of the Middle East, most notably the Carthaginians, with whom the Romans fought a long series of wars (the Punic Wars) from 264 BC until 146 BC. Eventually vanquishing the Carthaginians, Rome overran dozens or hundreds of other provinces, bringing hundreds of thousands of slaves flooding onto the Italian peninsula. This created unmanageable economic inequities, leading to a series of revolts, coup d'etats and civil wars. These culminated in a disastrous conflict (49-46 BC) that brought Julius Caesar to power. The assassination of Caesar (44 BC) pitched Rome back into civil war, and this war, after many years, brought to power Rome's greatest ruler, the Emperor Augustus.

Augustus made every possible effort to find and train a worthy successor, but failed to do so, leaving the empire in the hands of Tiberius, who was very competent, but vicious and brutal, and then the infamous Caligula. Still, the Julio-Claudian dynasty (founded by Augustus or, if you prefer, Julius Caesar) lasted until the death of Nero in 68 AD.

As an empire, Rome reached the zenith of its power in the years 100 to 180 AD, under the rulers known as the Five Good Emperors (Nerva, Trajan, Hadrian, Antoninus Pius, and Marcus Aurelius.) As these emperors had no sons, they were able to "adopt" sons, and thus were able to choose successors who were equal to the task of commanding an empire. They also adopted the practice of "sharing" the throne, creating orderly transitions of power, and also allowing the younger emperor to learn from the elder.

Marcus Aurelius, unfortunately, had a son, Commodus, who was lazy, vain, stupid and corrupt. After Commodus, Rome slipped back into the pattern of selecting emperors by a combination of war, assassination, birthright, and the whims of the Praetorian Guard. This lasted a hundred years, order being finally restored by Diocletian, who gained power in 285 AD. Diocletian put the empire, which appeared to be almost finished, back into sustainable condition for another century. After 400 AD the Roman Empire divided into an Eastern and a Western empire, and then into ever smaller and less powerful units, often at war with one another.

The History of the Jeffrey MacDonald Case in 10 Words
MacDonald's family was murdered in 1970. MacDonald is in prison.

The History of the Jeffrey MacDonald Case in 25 Words
Dr. Jeffrey MacDonald's wife and two daughters were murdered in 1970. MacDonald was convicted in 1979, and remains in prison today, still proclaiming his innocence.

The History of the Jeffrey MacDonald Case in 50 Words
About 3 AM on February 17, 1970, Colette MacDonald and her two daughters, Kristen and Kimberly, were murdered in their apartment at Fort Bragg, North Carolina. Jeffrey MacDonald was legally exonerated in October, 1970, but was convicted of the murders in 1979. Still proclaiming his innocence, he remains in prison.

The History of the Jeffrey MacDonald Case in 100 Words
About 3 AM on February 17, 1970, Colette MacDonald and her daughters, Kristen and Kimberly, were murdered in their apartment at Fort Bragg, North Carolina. Jeffrey MacDonald, husband and father of the victims, survived the attack, which he blamed on a home invasion by a group of hippies. Macdonald was exonerated in 1970, but due mostly to the persistence and determination of his in-laws, Freddy and Mildred Kassab, was brought to trial in 1979, and was convicted. Still proclaiming his innocence, he remains in prison. Many books have been written about the case, and many people believe MacDonald is innocent.

The History of the Jeffrey MacDonald Case in 200 Words
About 3 AM on February 17, 1970, Colette MacDonald and her daughters, Kristen and Kimberly, were murdered in their apartment at Fort Bragg, North Carolina. Dr. Jeffrey MacDonald survived the attack, which he blamed on a home invasion by a group of knife-wielding hippies.

The first investigation was slipshod. Investigators decided that MacDonald had committed the crime, and brought him before a military preliminary hearing in October, 1970. The officer in charge of that hearing not only cleared MacDonald, but declared flatly that MacDonald had not committed the crime.

MacDonald, however, alienated his in-laws, Freddy and Mildred Kassab, who campaigned to have him prosecuted. He appeared on the Dick Cavett show, national television, and left Cavett and many of the viewers convinced that he was guilty. He loudly and repeatedly charged the military with bungling the investigation, greatly annoying those who believed he had gotten by with murder. MacDonald was indicted in 1975 in a civilian court, pursuant to charges filed by Freddy Kassab. He was put on trial in 1979, and was convicted of the murders.

Still proclaiming his innocence, he remains imprisoned. Many books have been written about the case, and many people believe that MacDonald is innocent.

The History of the Jeffrey MacDonald Case in 500 Words

About 3 AM on February 17, 1970, Colette MacDonald and her daughters, Kristen and Kimberly, were stabbed to death in their apartment at Fort Bragg, North Carolina. Dr. Jeffrey MacDonald survived, and blamed the attack on a home invasion by hippies.

The investigation was slipshod. Investigators decided that MacDonald had committed the crime, and brought him before a military preliminary hearing in October, 1970. The officer in charge of that hearing not only cleared MacDonald, but declared flatly that MacDonald had not committed the crime.

Dr. MacDonald, immensely intelligent and charming, went on the offensive after his hearing, loudly and repeatedly accusing the military of bungling the investigation of the crime. His charm, however, seemed ill-suited to his position in life, and his publicity offensive backfired. He alienated his in-laws, Freddy and Mildred Kassab, who campaigned to have him prosecuted. His appearance on the Dick Cavett Show left Cavett and many of the viewers convinced that he was guilty. He annoyed the military officials who, he said, had bungled the case, which motivated them to look for other avenues to pursue prosecution. MacDonald was indicted in 1975 in a civilian court, pursuant to charges filed by Freddy Kassab. He went to trial in 1979, and was convicted of the murders.

As MacDonald and his lawyers were preparing for trial they were contacted by an author, the late Joe McGinniss, interested in writing a book about the case. McGinniss gave MacDonald and his attorneys reason to believe that the book would be pro-MacDonald, and McGinniss was allowed to join the defense team. McGinniss sat in with the defense on their meetings, on the preparation of witnesses, and actually lived with them during the trial; they were living in a fraternity house on the campus of North Carolina State. He was MacDonald's jogging partner and constant correspondent, and Mac-Donald allowed him complete access to his diaries and other papers.

McGinniss, however, decided that MacDonald was guilty, and after the conviction McGinniss wrote a book, *Fatal Vision*, concluding that MacDonald had been justly convicted. *Fatal Vision* became the Freddy Kassab story, the story of how Kassab had pursued justice for his murdered daughter.

McGinniss was not a good writer, and *Fatal Vision* is not a good book; it is rambling, repetitive, and often incoherent. It was, however, an immensely *successful* book, selling millions of copies and being made into an extremely successful mini-series starring Karl Malden as Freddy Kassab. The success of *Fatal Vision* so completely convinced the public of MacDonald's guilt that this assumption has formed a very high wall separating MacDonald from a full re-hearing of his case. MacDonald's key defense witness, Helena Stoeckley, died in 1983. MacDonald remains in prison today, although many, many people now believe him to be innocent. A recent book by the great Errol Morris (*A Wilderness of Error*) argues that he is in fact probably innocent, and was, at the least, wrongly convicted. An appeal by MacDonald is now in the hands of a judge.

———•———

YAZ AND BILLY

by Bill James

———·———

Billy Williams was born in 1938; Carl Yastrzemski, in 1939. Both players were left-handed hitters and right-handed throwers. Both players were left fielders, and both were primarily number three hitters. Both players were rookies in 1961. Billy Williams won the National League Rookie of the Year Award in 1961, although he had played a few games in 1959 and 1960, while Yaz was not mentioned in the Rookie of the Year voting in the American League, but did drive in 80 runs in his first season.

Both players are in the Hall of Fame. The Cubs are, in a sense, the Red Sox of the National League. There are five "old" franchises in each league which are still playing in the city where they were in 1950, 1940, 1930, 1920...the Cardinals, Reds, Pirates, Phillies and Cubs in the National League, the Tigers, Yankees, Indians, White Sox and Red Sox in the American League. All of those teams are playing in parks built in the last 25 years except the Cubs and Red Sox, in Wrigley and Fenway. At the time these men played, both parks were hitters' parks—Fenway the best hitter's park in the AL, Wrigley (at that time) the best hitter's park in the NL. Both players, in their careers, hit over .300 at home, nowhere near .300 on the road.

Both players came into organizations that were down and out, and both organizations re-emerged as competitive organizations in 1967—the Red Sox more dramatically, of course, but the Cubs by a wider margin. The Red Sox improved by 20 games in 1967, from 72 wins to 92; the Cubs improved by 28 games, from 59 wins to 87. Both organizations had losing records every year from 1961 through 1966, except that the Cubs did manage to go 82-80 in 1963, and both organizations had winning records every year 1967 through 1973.

169

The stats, in general, are close enough to be interchangeable. Yaz in his best season hit .326 with 44 homers, 121 RBI; Williams in his best season hit .322 with 42 homers, 129 RBI. Their best seasons are what Henry Aaron did every year. Their stats are interchangeable in every area except Games Played (Williams never missed a game) and walks, and even in walks, they're not radically different. Yaz had a period in the middle of his career where he had big walk numbers; Williams didn't. Otherwise, their walk rates are similar.

Both players are listed in the record books at 175 pounds. Because Williams was born in June of 1938, convention regards him as 23 years old in 1961, whereas Yaz, because he was born in August of 1939, is conventionally regarded as 21 years old in 1961, although Yaz was actually only 14 months younger than Williams. Using the conventional age system, this is a "best-ball" career for the two of them, a career for Billy Yastrzemski:

AGE	G	AB	R	H	2B	3B	HR	RBI	BB	SO	SB	Avg	OBA	SPct	OPS
21	148	583	71	155	31	6	11	80	50	96	6	.266	.324	.396	.721
22	160	**646**	99	191	43	6	19	94	66	82	7	.296	.363	.469	.832
23	151	570	91	183	40	3	14	68	95	72	8	.321	.418	.475	.894
24	159	618	94	184	22	8	22	91	70	72	9	.298	.369	.466	.835
25	133	494	78	154	**45**	3	20	72	70	58	7	.312	.395	.536	.932
26	**162**	645	100	201	39	2	33	98	59	84	10	.312	.370	.532	.901
27	161	579	112	189	31	4	**44**	121	91	69	10	.326	.418	**.622**	1.040
28	157	539	90	162	32	2	23	74	119	90	13	.301	.426	.495	.922
29	**162**	603	96	154	28	2	40	111	101	**91**	15	.255	.362	.507	.870
30	161	566	125	186	29	0	40	102	**128**	66	**23**	.329	**.452**	.592	**1.044**
31	163	642	103	188	33	**10**	21	95	59	70	3	.293	.355	.474	.828
32	161	636	**137**	**205**	34	4	42	**129**	72	65	7	.322	.391	.586	.977
33	157	594	86	179	27	5	28	93	77	44	7	.301	.383	.505	.888
34	150	574	95	191	34	6	37	122	62	59	3	**.333**	.398	.606	1.005
35	156	576	72	166	22	2	20	86	76	72	4	.288	.369	.437	.806
36	155	546	71	146	23	2	21	102	80	67	5	.267	.357	.432	.790
37	150	558	99	165	27	3	28	102	73	40	11	.296	.379	.505	.885
38	144	523	70	145	21	2	17	81	76	44	4	.277	.367	.423	.790
39	147	518	69	140	28	1	21	87	62	46	3	.270	.346	.450	.796
40	105	364	49	100	21	1	15	50	44	38	0	.275	.363	.462	.824
41	91	338	36	83	14	1	7	53	49	28	0	.246	.349	.355	.704
42	131	459	53	126	22	1	16	72	59	50	0	.275	.356	.431	.787
43	119	380	38	101	24	0	10	56	54	29	0	.266	.380	.408	.788
	3383	12551	1934	3694	670	74	549	2039	1692	1432	155	.294	.378	.491	.868

Bold Face marks the career highs. Can you walk through that and say which season is Yastrzemski's, and which is Williams'? This is the "leftover seasons" career, a career for the sprinter, Carl Williams:

AGE	G	AB	R	H	2B	3B	HR	RBI	BB	SO	SB	Avg	OBA	SPct	OPS
21	18	33	0	5	0	1	0	2	1	7	0	.152	.176	.212	.389
22	12	47	4	13	0	2	2	7	5	12	0	.277	.346	.489	.836
23	146	529	75	147	20	7	25	86	45	70	6	.278	.338	.484	.822
24	151	567	77	164	29	9	15	67	75	**90**	6	.289	.374	.451	.825
25	161	612	87	175	36	9	25	95	68	78	7	.286	.358	.497	.854
26	160	594	81	165	**39**	2	16	80	84	60	8	.278	.368	.431	.799
27	**164**	**645**	**115**	**203**	**39**	6	**34**	**108**	65	76	10	**.315**	.377	**.552**	**.929**
28	162	648	100	179	23	5	29	91	69	61	6	.276	.347	.461	.808
29	162	634	92	176	21	**12**	28	84	68	67	6	.278	.346	.481	.828
30	163	642	91	185	30	8	30	98	48	53	4	.288	.336	.500	.836
31	148	508	75	129	21	2	15	70	**106**	60	8	.254	.381	.392	.772
32	125	455	70	120	18	2	12	68	67	44	5	.264	.357	.391	.748
33	152	540	82	160	25	4	19	95	105	58	9	.296	.407	.463	.870
34	148	515	93	155	25	2	15	79	104	48	**12**	.301	**.414**	.445	.859
35	149	543	91	146	30	1	14	60	87	67	8	.269	.371	.405	.776
36	117	404	55	113	22	0	16	68	67	44	4	.280	.382	.453	.835
37	155	520	68	127	20	1	23	81	76	68	0	.244	.349	.419	.769
38	120	351	36	74	12	0	11	41	58	44	4	.211	.320	.339	.659
	2413	8787	1292	2436	410	73	329	1280	1198	1007	103	.277	.363	.453	.816

Most of you will assume, going into our analysis, that Yastrzemski was a greater player than Williams. Let me be the Devil's Advocate. While both Yaz and Williams played in hitter's parks, Yaz got more help from Fenway than Williams did from Wiggley. Yastrzemski's career OPS in his home park is six points higher than Williams (.905 to .899)—but in road parks, Williams was 29 points ahead (.808 to .779).

Yastrzemski's season in 1967, because the Red Sox won the pennant, because it was such a dramatic pennant race and because it was such a surprise, has entered the mythology of the game. Because the Cubs did not quite win in 1970 and 1972, and because it was not Boston, Williams' seasons did not get the same standing. The Cubs finished second both seasons (1970 and 1972), and Williams was second in the MVP voting both seasons. Finishing second is not the same as winning; I understand that. But is it Williams' fault that the Cubs relief ace in 1970 was Phil Regan (5-9 with a 4.74

ERA, 12 Saves)? If Carlton Fisk had been their catcher rather than Randy Hundley, the Cubs would have won their division both years.

Yaz had an easier path to the Hall of Fame because

1) MVP Awards unlock the door to Cooperstown, and
2) Yaz hung on to get 3,000 career hits, and well past.

"Hanging on" is not greatness, says my friend Marty, who is a Cubs fan. The Cubs and Red Sox both had talent-productive cycles in the early 1960s, which matured in 1967. The Red Sox had a second talent boom in the mid-1970s, with Rice and Lynn and Evans. The Cubs after 1966 stopped producing talent, which forced them to trade off Williams (and Santo, and Ferguson Jenkins) to try to stay competitive. Is that Billy Williams fault?

(Actually, the statement that Yaz had an easier path to the Hall of Fame is negotiable. Yaz went into the Hall of Fame in his first year of eligibility, whereas Williams was rejected five times before he was elected in 1987. However, because Williams retired much younger, Williams was actually younger than Yaz was at the time he was elected to Cooperstown.)

Yastrzemski stole more bases. Williams had a better stolen base percentage, and grounded into significantly fewer double plays.

OK, let's get into the Win Shares and Loss Shares. Since both players were rookies in 1961, I'm going to compare them through calendar seasons (rather than same age), remembering that Williams is fourteen months older. Williams got a late-season callup in 1959, was declared "Not Ready," got another late-season callup in 1960 and did better:

Year	Player	Age	G	AB	HR	RBI	AVG	SLG	OBA	OPS	Batting W	Batting L	Fielding W	Fielding L	Total W	Total L	Pct
1959	Billy	21	18	33	0	2	.152	.212	.176	.389	0	2	0	0	0	2	.000
1960	Billy	22	12	47	2	7	.277	.489	.346	.836	1	1	0	0	1	1	.578

In 1961, as I mentioned, Williams was the National League's Rookie of the Year, while Yastrzemski was in the lineup all year for Boston, although he didn't really do much:

Year	Player	Age	G	AB	HR	RBI	AVG	SLG	OBA	OPS	Batting W	Batting L	Fielding W	Fielding L	Total W	Total L	Pct
1961	Billy	23	146	529	25	86	.278	.484	.338	.822	13	9	1	6	14	15	.490
1961	Yaz	21	148	583	11	80	.266	.396	.324	.721	10	15	1	6	11	21	.351

Williams was Rookie of the Year in 1961, and justified that selection with a Hall of Fame career, but—like most Rookies of the Year—he was really just kind of an average player as a rookie. He was a pretty good hitter, not a really good hitter, but a below-average fielder at a defensive position that doesn't have the highest expectations on the field. Yaz, with his low on-base percentage and sub-.400 slugging, was just getting acquainted with the American League. He finished strong, hitting .320 with 4 homers in September, 1961. In 1962 both players were better.

From 1962 to 1966 both players were above-average every season, but from 1961 to 1966 Williams was the better player every year. It's not just the fact that Williams was older, and ahead that way; Williams in 1964-1965 was substantially ahead of Yastrzemski, more than an "age-step." In 1963 it is actually debatable who was ahead. Yastrzemski won his first American League batting title and also led the American League in Walks, Doubles and On Base Percentage, but Williams is still ahead of him by the value formula (2 Wins minus Losses), which I am using to sort the players...it's a kind of a shorthand WAR (Wins Against Replacement). I suspect most WAR formulas would put Yastrzemski in front in that season:

Year	Player	Age	G	AB	HR	RBI	AVG	SLG	OBA	OPS	Batting W	Batting L	Fielding W	Fielding L	Total W	Total L	Total Pct
1962	Billy	24	159	618	22	91	.298	.466	.369	.835	16	10	2	5	18	15	.543
1962	Yaz	22	160	646	19	94	.296	.469	.363	.832	16	11	2	5	18	16	.532
1963	Billy	25	161	612	25	95	.286	.497	.358	.854	20	6	5	4	24	10	.705
1963	Yaz	23	151	570	14	68	.321	.475	.418	.894	20	3	2	4	22	7	.764
1964	Billy	26	162	645	33	98	.312	.532	.370	.901	21	5	3	6	23	11	.676
1964	Yaz	24	151	567	15	67	.289	.451	.374	.825	15	9	2	4	17	14	.555
1965	Billy	27	164	645	34	108	.315	.552	.377	.929	22	3	4	5	26	8	.764
1965	Yaz	25	133	494	20	72	.312	.536	.395	.932	16	4	1	5	17	9	.645
1966	Billy	28	162	648	29	91	.276	.461	.347	.808	18	9	3	5	21	14	.603
1966	Yaz	26	160	594	16	80	.278	.431	.368	.799	15	10	2	5	17	15	.527

In '62 they're basically tied, with almost the same batting averages, on base and slugging percentages. In '63 they're different but similar in value. From '64 through '66 Yastrzemski didn't keep up. In 1964 Billy Williams started out red hot, hitting .413 through June

5, in the lineup every game. There was some talk about whether he could hit .400. "What the *****," he told a reporter. "I haven't hit .300 yet." He faded in mid-summer but was over .300 at the finish line in '64 and in '65, hitting twice as many homers as Yaz in those years.

Through 1966 we credit Billy Williams with a career won-lost record of 128-76, whereas Yastrzemski is just 102-82. 128-76 is barely a Hall of Fame level of performance. 102-82 is substantially short of a Hall of Fame course. There is a point there which can be stated in English and defended in English or math: through 1966, Carl Yastrzemski certainly did not appear to be headed to Cooperstown. In 1966 he hit .278 with 16 homers, 80 RBI. Even in the 1960s, those aren't Hall of Fame numbers. He was 26 years old then, and his career high in home runs was 20. He had never driven in or scored 100 runs. With the exception of one season, his career high in RBI was 80. Yes, it's the 1960s, but from 1961 through 1966 there were 62 seasons in which a player scored 100 runs, and 74 in which a player drove in 100 runs. Yaz wasn't on either list. He was not playing at a Hall of Fame level.

Let's deal with Yaz's defense. Yastrzemski won seven Gold Gloves, and his ability to play The Wall at Fenway Park was—and is—legendary. We're not giving him great defensive won-lost records. Isn't it possible, people will ask…people always say this as if they were the first person ever to think of such a thing, and you're not allowed to kick them in the balls anymore…isn't it possible that Yastrzemski's defensive ratings are hurt by the fact that he played left field in Fenway Park, where:

a) The left field area is very small, and
b) The left fielder has to play 20 feet closer to the batter, whether he wants to or not, which gives him less time to react.

Well, yes, of course it is possible. Defensive statistics are tricky, and our ability to adjust for things like park effects in fielding is very limited because we don't have the detailed fielding information that we do for hitters. On the other hand, it is not clear or obvious that my numbers are shorting him. In my method, every fielder competes with the value of every other fielder. The left fielder competes with the shortstop—just as he does at bat. The left fielder usually wins the competition with the bat, usually loses the competition as to fielding value. Most left fielders have defensive winning percentages well below .500.

Billy Williams and Carl Yastrzemski, as we can see, are profoundly similar in many different ways. Billy Williams' defensive won-lost record, as a rookie, was 1-6. Carl Yastrzemski's was 1-6. Billy Williams' defensive won-lost record in his second season was 2-5. Carl Yastrzemski's was 2-5. Isn't it possible that they really are of about the same value in the field, as they are on so many other scales—particularly early in their careers?

Let's set that argument aside, and let us *assume* that Yastrzemski's defense is being under-evaluated by this method. I think... I sincerely believe...that it very probably is. On the other hand, Fangraphs...if I understand the information on their site correctly, which is always a gamble...but if I understand what they're saying, they have Yastrzemski rated defensively at +23 runs in 1966, +23 runs in 1967, and +25 runs in 1968. I would rather try to defend my defensive ratings than *those* defensive ratings. I think it is improbable that Yastrzemski in his prime was 24 runs a year better than an average defensive left fielder.

But who knows? Let's just agree that Yaz is probably better in the field than my numbers are giving him credit for, at least in some seasons, and then we'll return to that issue at the end of the comparison. We had worked through 1966, and through 1966 Williams was outplaying Yastrzemski pretty much every season. In 1967, the year that both the Cubs and Red Sox re-emerged as competitive teams, Yaz suddenly vaulted ahead of Williams—and everybody else in baseball:

Year	Player	Age	G	AB	HR	RBI	AVG	SLG	OBA	OPS	Batting		Fielding		Total		
											W	L	W	L	W	L	Pct
1967	Yaz	27	161	579	44	121	.326	.622	.418	1.040	26	-3	3	4	29	1	.983
1967	Billy	29	162	634	28	84	.278	.481	.346	.828	20	7	4	5	24	11	.676
1968	Yaz	28	157	539	23	74	.301	.495	.426	.922	26	-4	3	5	29	1	.975
1968	Billy	30	163	642	30	98	.288	.500	.336	.836	20	7	4	5	23	12	.661
1969	Billy	31	163	642	21	95	.293	.474	.355	.828	17	9	4	4	21	13	.619
1969	Yaz	29	162	603	40	111	.255	.507	.362	.870	18	8	2	5	20	13	.616
1970	Yaz	30	161	566	40	102	.329	.592	.452	1.044	24	-1	2	4	27	3	.910
1970	Billy	32	161	636	42	129	.322	.586	.391	.977	19	6	4	4	23	10	.698

In 1967, 1968 and 1970 Yastrzemski played at a level that Billy Williams would never reach. In those three seasons Yastrzemski was at the level of Mays, Aaron, Pujols, Musial, Joe Morgan...the Hall of Fame's inner circle. He had the very high on base percentages, in those years, that mark the almost unbeatable players. With the exception of those three seasons, neither Yastrzemski or Williams was ever at that level. In 1969, when Yaz's average slipped to .255, the two of them were basically even...we have Billy an inch ahead, but again, there's that issue with the accurate evaluation of Yastrzemski's defense.

Yaz was sensational, but Billy Williams wasn't chopped bologna in those years, either; we have him with won-lost contributions of 24-11, 23-12, 20-13 and 23-10. That's a Hall of Fame level of performance if you do it every year, and since 1963 he had been doing it every year. Through 1970, then, Yastrzemski's career won-lost contribution was 208-99—which is very much a Hall of Fame level of performance—while Williams was at 219-122. Yastrzemski had pulled ahead.

After hitting 40 homers a year from 1967 to 1970 (basically), Yastrzemski dropped in 1971 to .254 with 15 homers. Billy Williams continued to roll along just as before, and in fact Williams' best season was still ahead of him:

Year	Player	Age	G	AB	HR	RBI	AVG	SLG	OBA	OPS	Batting		Fielding		Total		
											W	L	W	L	W	L	Pct
1971	Billy	33	157	594	28	93	.301	.505	.383	.888	19	5	3	5	22	11	.679
1971	Yaz	31	148	508	15	70	.254	.392	.381	.772	14	8	2	5	17	13	.564
1972	Billy	34	150	574	37	122	.333	.606	.398	1.005	22	0	4	4	26	4	.868
1972	Yaz	32	125	455	12	68	.264	.391	.357	.748	13	7	1	5	15	12	.554

Yastrzemski in 1971-72 went back to being the player he had been before 1967—an above average player, but not much more than that. Whether Williams' best season was 1970 or 1972 depends on what you look at. As I mentioned, he was second in the MVP voting both years. In 1970 Williams scored 137 runs, which actually is the most runs scored by any major league player in any season in the 1950s, 1960s or 1970s. He had more homers and RBI in 1970 than in 1972.

1972 was a strike-shortened season, which took the edge off of Williams' numbers. Williams played in 1,117 consecutive games, which was the National League record at the time—the Cal Ripken/Lou Gehrig record—since broken by Steve Garvey. By 1972 he had given up playing every game, although he still played almost every game; anyway he had 10% more plate appearances in 1970 than in 1972, which makes the counting stats look better in 1970. But

Williams' OPS was higher in 1972 than in 1970, whereas overall offensive numbers in 1972 were way down from 1970. The National League ERA was 4.05 in 1970, 3.45 in 1972. The league OPS was .721 in 1970, .680 in 1972. There were 8,771 runs scored in the National League in 1970, 7,265 in 1972. Compared to the league, what Williams did in 1972 is much more impressive than what he had done in 1970, and also, the raw park effect for Wiggley was much higher in 1970 than in 1972.

Anyway, Williams' by 1972 had a career won-lost contribution of 268-137; Yastrzemski, of 239-123. Williams was back ahead. From 1973 on, both players were post-prime. Yastrzemski had a bounce-back season in 1973 and stayed near that (1973) level for ten years after that. From 1973 on, Williams never had a season in which he was Yastrzemski's equal:

Year	Player	Age	G	AB	HR	RBI	AVG	SLG	OBA	OPS	Batting W	L	Fielding W	L	Total W	L	Pct
1973	Yaz	33	152	540	19	95	.296	.463	.407	.870	18	5	3	4	21	8	.716
1973	Billy	35	156	576	20	86	.288	.438	.369	.806	15	9	3	5	19	13	.587
1974	Yaz	34	148	515	15	79	.301	.445	.414	.859	19	3	5	4	24	6	.785
1974	Billy	36	117	404	16	68	.280	.453	.382	.835	13	4	1	4	14	8	.632
1975	Yaz	35	149	543	14	60	.269	.405	.371	.776	14	9	5	2	19	12	.621
1975	Billy	37	155	520	23	81	.244	.419	.341	.760	16	7	0	4	16	11	.597
1976	Yaz	36	155	546	21	102	.267	.432	.357	.790	15	9	4	5	19	13	.587
1976	Billy	38	120	351	11	41	.211	.339	.320	.659	8	8	0	3	8	11	.415

Traded to Oakland in 1975, Williams had one good season as a DH, then one bad season as a DH, and retired after the 1976 campaign. From 1962 to 1975, Billy Williams was a very good player every year, with very moderate ups and downs. He retired with a career won-lost contribution of 324-180, which is certainly a Hall of Fame level of performance. At the time that Williams' retired, Yaz was at 322-163. Yaz then played on for seven more seasons, and was an above-average player throughout those seven years:

Year	Player	Age	G	AB	HR	RBI	AVG	SLG	OBA	OPS	Batting W	Batting L	Fielding W	Fielding L	Total W	Total L	Pct
1977	Yaz	37	150	558	28	102	.296	.505	.372	.877	16	8	4	4	20	11	.643
1978	Yaz	38	144	523	17	81	.277	.423	.367	.790	15	8	3	4	17	12	.598
1979	Yaz	39	147	518	21	87	.270	.450	.346	.796	12	10	2	4	14	14	.507
1980	Yaz	40	105	364	15	50	.275	.462	.350	.812	10	6	1	3	11	9	.537
1981	Yaz	41	91	338	7	53	.246	.355	.338	.693	7	8	1	2	8	10	.436
1982	Yaz	42	131	459	16	72	.275	.431	.358	.789	11	8	1	3	12	11	.508
1983	Yaz	43	119	380	10	56	.266	.408	.359	.767	9	7	0	2	9	10	.490

With a career won-lost contribution of 413-240, Yastrzemski far exceeds the minimum standards of the Hall of Fame and easily outdistances Billy Williams. Let's run the career Win Shares and Loss Shares for each player:

	BILLY WILLIAMS						
	Batting		Fielding		Total		
Year	W	L	W	L	W	L	Pct
1959	0	2	0	0	0	2	.000
1960	1	1	0	0	1	1	.578
1961	13	9	1	6	14	15	.490
1962	16	10	2	5	18	15	.543
1963	20	6	5	4	24	10	.705
1964	21	5	3	6	23	11	.676
1965	22	3	4	5	26	8	.764
1966	18	9	3	5	21	14	.603
1967	20	7	4	5	24	11	.676
1968	20	7	4	5	23	12	.661
1969	17	9	4	4	21	13	.619
1970	19	6	4	4	23	10	.698
1971	19	5	3	5	22	11	.679
1972	22	0	4	4	26	4	.868
1973	15	9	3	5	19	13	.587
1974	13	4	1	4	14	8	.632
1975	16	7	0	4	16	11	.597
1976	8	8	0	3	8	11	.415
	279	106	45	74	324	180	.643
	.725		.378		.643		

CARL YASTRZEMSKI							
	Batting		Fielding		Total		
Year	W	L	W	L	W	L	Pct
1961	10	15	1	6	11	21	.351
1962	16	11	2	5	18	16	.532
1963	20	3	2	4	22	7	.764
1964	15	9	2	4	17	14	.555
1965	16	4	1	5	17	9	.645
1966	15	10	2	5	17	15	.527
1967	26	-3	3	4	29	1	.983
1968	26	-4	3	5	29	1	.975
1969	18	8	2	5	20	13	.616
1970	24	-1	2	4	27	3	.910
1971	14	8	2	5	17	13	.564
1972	13	7	1	5	15	12	.554
1973	18	5	3	4	21	8	.716
1974	19	3	5	4	24	6	.785
1975	14	9	5	2	19	12	.621
1976	15	9	4	5	19	13	.587
1977	16	8	4	4	20	11	.643
1978	15	8	3	4	17	12	.598
1979	12	10	2	4	14	14	.507
1980	10	6	1	3	11	9	.537
1981	7	8	1	2	8	10	.436
1982	11	8	1	3	12	11	.508
1983	9	7	0	2	9	10	.490
	361	147	53	93	413	240	.633
		.710		.362		.633	

Getting back to the issue of Yastrzemski's defensive evaluation…Carl Yastrzemski in his career played 1,917 games in left field, 764 at first base, 411 as a DH. He had games at other positions as well, including a season's worth in center field, but those were his three primary defensive positions.

It is almost impossible for a player who is a first baseman, a left fielder and a DH to make a defensive contribution equal to that of a shortstop, a catcher or a center field. It's not 100% impossible, if you're Keith Hernandez or somebody, but as a rule…a first baseman, a center fielder or a left fielder is not asked to match the defensive contribution of the second baseman or the right fielder. That's what defensive wins and losses measure: the defensive contribution of *this* player compared to that of an average player. For a DH, that's always .000, and for a left fielder or first baseman, it's normally in the .400 range.

Let's agree that Yastrzemski's defensive winning percentage

a) shouldn't be .362, and
b) should be higher than Williams'.

What should it be? Williams is at .378. Should it be .390, .400?

Let's say it is .410. I doubt that it should be .410, but let's say it is. If it was .410, that would make Yastrzemski's overall won-lost contribution 420-233 (.643) rather than 413-240 (.633). My point is that, while we may indeed have shorted Yastrzemski as a defensive player because of Fenway Park, it's not a big deal. At .643 he would have the same overall winning percentage as Billy Williams, in a longer career. With or without the adjustment, Yastrzemski still ranks ahead of Williams in the Parade of the Immortals.

———·———

Opinions, Philosophy and Ideas

by Bill James

———

What is the difference between an opinion and an idea?

I generally despise opinions—yours, mine, and especially somebody else's. I do not listen to talk shows, sports or otherwise, and I don't like to allow myself to give my opinions in print, although I do of course. When people ask for my opinion about something, I will try to invent a way to approach the question quantitatively and objectively, rather than simply giving my opinion.

I am, on the other hand, entirely driven by ideas. It occurred to me then to ask: what exactly is the difference between an idea and an opinion?

Back up one...what is the difference between "philosophy" and "*A philosophy.*"

I don't know anything about philosophy, but I am consumed with the effort to find better ways to think about problems. I recognize the contradiction. No doubt I should have educated myself about philosophy. I didn't. I'm an ignoramus; just ignore me.

"Philosophy" is the search for truth, the effort to understand the true nature of the problem. Philosophers often reach for the true nature of the universe, which may be why we ignore them; we all know, intuitively, that no one can figure out the true nature of the universe. Let us say that philosophy is the effort to understand the nature of a problem.

"*A philosophy,*" on the other hand, is an organized way of thinking about a problem. We all develop A political philosophy, A philosophy about raising children, A philosophy about education, A philosophy about sports. A philosophy is the back-end result of philosophy; A philosophy is the excrement of philosophy. When there is no food value left in food, your body gets rid of it. When you *stop* trying to figure out the true nature of the problem, then you have *A philosophy* about the problem. *A philosophy* is what you have when you're done thinking.

I despise opinions because opinions are barriers to thought. An "opinion" is formed by the intersection of a live topic (Roger Clemens' acquittal, the newest TV show, the current political controversy) with A general philosophy. I don't believe in *any* general philosophy, as a rule, because I don't think that anyone understands the world or that anyone's way of thinking systematically about the world holds up to scrutiny. Any moron can see what is wrong with either liberalism or conservatism, if he merely has the intellectual integrity to admit it, just as any moron can easily see the flaws in Christianity, Judaism or atheism. We can't move on from there to *A philosophy* that does work, however, because we're simply not smart enough to construct one. The world is billions of times more complicated than the human mind; therefore, none of us can develop *A philosophy* that consistently explains new and diverse phenomenon. There is no doubt a name for this philosophy.

An idea, on the other hand, has no first object (such as Clemens, the new TV show or the current political uproar), and it has no philosophy. An idea is formed not from *A philosophy* and an issue, but from a question and some avenue of thought running into that question. How do I measure this? What is the value in this? What is the potential in this?

People sign on to liberalism and conservatism not because they are too stupid to see their flaws; no one is that stupid. People sign on to them because they cannot stand to live with unanswered questions. The source of all anxiety is unanswered questions. We need answers. We prefer bad answers to the lack of an answer. The court system will sometimes convict innocent people of terrible crimes, simply because they cannot stand for the crime to go unpunished, for the riddle to go unanswered. The answers offered by liberalism and conservatism, or by stoicism and cynicism for that matter, are childish and uniformly ugly—but they are answers. They provide us with a way to walk up to a problem, pick an avenue and walk away from the problem; thus, they carry us away from the horrible problem of not knowing what to think.

That's my philosophy. You're welcome.

COUPLE OF GREAT OLD BASEBALL STORIES

by Bill James

MY WORST BLUNDER
Famous Bonehead Plays
on Major League Diamonds
Explained by Leading Baseball Players to

Hugh S. Fullerton

ED KONETCHY
**First Baseman, St. Louis Cardinals,
who is considered by many experts
as the Best First Baseman in the Game Today.**

You may think it odd, but the fact is that I won a ball game with what I think was the worst mistake I ever made. Maybe I wouldn't admit that if it had lost the game, except to fellows I know well enough, but it was. Lots of times I read how someone makes a boneheaded play when I know it was a good play, and lots of times I read about them making good plays that are good plays only because they got away with them. Any play is a good play as long as it is a help toward winning a game, and any play is a rotten play if it loses a ball game. The fans want to win, and if you win they don't care for the science of it. I'll let them call me a bone head every day if we can win ball games by it.

We were playing the Chicago club early in 1911, and fighting them off their feet in the series. It was a fierce fight all the way, as every game of the series was, and the score was close when we came down to the end. We were tied, and neither had scored many runs, but late in the game Chicago got a runner to second base with one out, and we were battling to keep them from scoring the winning run. Hofman was at bat and I was watching closely to see what our pitcher was handing up to him, and playing a little bit closer to the bag than usual because of Hofman's speed in coming down to first. He hit the ball a mile a minute, almost over the corner of the base, and as I saw it coming I knew it was up to me to stop that ball or the game was gone. It didn't look as if anyone had a chance to reach the ball, but I jumped over and made a slap at it with my mitt. The ball jumped up just in time to hit the edge of the mitt hard, and I knew I had blocked its force and that it was only a base hit instead of the triple it would have been had it passed the mitt. I really didn't know where the ball was, but saw it rolling slowly back of me into right field.

That far I had made a nice play and a lucky stop. I jumped after the ball, and in doing so I must have lost my head. I knew the runner was certain to beat the ball to first. He was ahead of Sallee, who was coming over to cover first, when I picked up the ball, and there wasn't a chance to catch him. My play, without doubt, was to get that ball back to the plate to prevent the runner from second trying to score, and if I could hold him at third, which ought to have been easy, we still would have a chance to cut off the runner at the plate or try for a double play. I was so anxious and rattled that I leaped on the ball and cut loose at full speed to first. Sallee was covering as fast as he could, but the way I threw he couldn't have caught the ball any more than he could catch a cannon ball. The ball went past him like a flash, struck the dirt, bounded straight into the catcher's hands, and the runner who was trying to score from second was out by ten feet at the plate.

It took us a long time to win that game. We tied in eleven innings that day, tied when we tried to play it off, and we finally won it in late September.

I used to like to do "Tracers" in some of my old books, in which I would pick up an old story like this and try to backtrack and find the original facts. Since I saw this story about a game in 1911 and Retrosheet has good accounts of the 1911 season available now, I thought I would try to see if I could find the exact game in which this "accidental" good play occurred.

We have lots of facts to deal with here; the year is given, the time of the year (early in the season), details about the game, the hitter, the inning, the pitcher...there's a lot to work with there. To jump to the conclusion, because I don't know how else I would do this, it does not appear that there is any series of events that is a close match for Konetchy's account of them. I don't doubt that some play very much like this did occur somewhere, sometime, but Konetchy has pretty clearly made one story out of several memorable but unrelated incidents.

Saying "we tied in eleven innings that day," is pretty clearly a reference to the game of April 12, 1911, which was opening day of the season at the West Side Grounds. The Cubs and Cardinals did play to an eleven-inning tie on that date, and Sallee did pitch. It matches Konetchy's description of "early in the season"; you can't get any earlier in the season than opening day.

However, at least according to the Retrosheet account, there was no play in the game which bears substantial similarities to the play described by Konetchy. Solly Hofman did play in the game, but went 0-for-5 and did not reach base. Konetchy did throw out a runner at home plate in that game, but it was on a relay throw from the outfield, early in the game, and Sallee would not have been covering first on the play.

Konetchy says that when they tried to re-play the game it ended in another tie. The Cubs and Cardinals did play another game later in the series (April 15) which, again, ended in a tie. This could have been a make-up game for the earlier tie; I don't know. But again, there was no play in that game that accords with Konetchy's account. Sallee did not appear in that game, Hofman did not get a hit, and Konetchy did not have an assist, did not throw out a runner at the plate or at any other base. There just isn't anything in the play-by-play for either game that could be mistaken for Konetchy's story.

As to Konetchy's memory that the Cardinals won the game on the second makeup try...well, if you say so. The Cardinals didn't play in Chicago again after that game until mid-August; they played three games in Chicago in mid-August, but lost them all. They were back in Chicago from September 3 to September 6—not "late" September, but it was at least September—and played six games against Chicago in four days, of which we would assume that two were makeup games for the games in the first series which had ended in a tie. However, the Cubs won four of the six games, and the Cubs won both second games of double headers, which would be the most likely makeup games under the re-scheduling rules that I am familiar with. However, some re-scheduling practices at that time may have been radically different, so I wouldn't place much faith in my assumptions about that.

Again, there does not appear to be any event in this six-game series which is a good match for Konetchy's memory. Sallee was injured and did not appear in the series. In the first game Retrosheet has no play by play, but Konetchy did not have an assist and Hofman does not appear likely to have batted with anyone on base at any point in the game.

The second game—again no play by play—Konetchy did not have an assist, and the Cubs lost.

In the third game we have play by play, and there is no event even broadly comparable to Konetchy's story.

In the fourth game we have no play by play, but

a) the Cubs won,
b) Hofman didn't have a hit, and
c) Konetchy didn't have an assist.

If the fifth game we have play by play, and there is, again, no similar event.

In the sixth game we have play by play. The Cubs won the game 9 to 0, and there is nothing in the game that resembles Konetchy's story.

Again, I don't question that something like this happened, sometime, somewhere. But it does not appear to have occurred where and when Konetchy remembers it as happening, which is 1911 against Chicago. I also checked the St. Louis/Chicago games that were played in St. Louis. Nothing.

Since I'm here, I'll mention some other stuff about Konetchy that I found while trying to track this down. First, there is a story told repeatedly about Konetchy's entry into minor league baseball. The essence of the story is that Konetchy attended a game as a fan and was pressed into service by the home team because of an injury. He played so well that the manager told him to report for practice the next day, but Konetchy responded that he couldn't do it. He was being paid $12 a week to work in a candy store, and he didn't want to give up the job. The manager contacted the candy store owner and arranged to "borrow" Big Ed on a regular basis.

Second, there are constant references to Konetchy's ability in the field, and one or two comparisons of Konetchy to Hal Chase, who was of course the standard of fielding excellence at first base in that era.

Third, I found an account of a double play that Konetchy was involved in against the New York Giants in 1910 that went 3-2-3-2. With the bases loaded and Red Ames batting, Ames hit the ball to Konetchy, who fired home for the forceout. The catcher threw back to first, trying to make a 3-2-3 double play, but the throw to first was too late. The runner from second, however, rounded third and headed for home; Konetchy threw back to the plate and was credited with both assists on a double play.

Fourth, Konetchy was a bit of a character, and there are quite a few human interest stories about him. My favorite involves a vaudeville house that Konetchy owned in St. Louis, which he personally managed during the off season. One time he hired a three-person act, but the act was terrible, and after a few days he called them into his office and told them he was going to have to put them on waivers. It's a joke, you see; you ask waivers on a baseball player when he is being given his release. There weren't any "waivers" in vaudeville.

The other thing that strikes me about the anecdote told to Fullerton is how clean and modern the language is. A lot of the sports writing of 1911 is convoluted and uses stilted, archaic jargon. This one is so natural-sounding that the only thing that jars you is the use of the term "mitts"; we still occasionally describe a first baseman's glove as a "mitt", but, in the context above, a player today would just say "glove", not "mitt". Otherwise...it sounds about the same as if it had been told yesterday.

Here's one more story I found.

> Perhaps the most remarkable catch made anywhere during the season of 1910 was made by Carlisle of the Vernon team of the Pacific coast league on the San Francisco grounds early in October. The catch was made possible because it started in a joking tribute by Carlisle to the hitting prowess of "Ping" Bodie, the slugging outfielder of the Frisco team, who came near breaking world's records for home run hits during the season.
>
> The San Francisco grounds are situated low, and surrounded by great fences, some of them as tall as the three-story houses that adjoin the park.

At points the fences are nearly fifty feet high, yet Bodie kept driving the ball over fences, signs and high screens until it got to be a regular thing and a source of joking among the fans and players alike. The Vernon team came down from the north with the Frisco team, and they stopped to play a series on the Mission street grounds. It happened that while the team was away painters had been putting some new lettering on signs high above the fence, and one tall ladder remained propped against the fence in right center field. The ladder was left there, and after Vernon had batted and failed to score, Carlisle, jogging out to his position, saw the ladder, and thought of a joke. Two were out when "Ping," the hero of Frisco, came to bat. Carlisle jogged back to the fence and, climbing about twenty feet up the ladder, turned his face toward the field. The bleacher crowd appreciated his tribute to Bodie's hitting power and laughed and cheered, and the crowd in the stands took up the applause. Bodie swung wickedly upon the first ball pitched. Carlisle, thinking he had carried the joke far enough, was descending the ladder, when he saw the ball coming toward the fence, far above his head. He turned, scrambled ten feet up the ladder, clung to a round with one hand and, stretching out the other, caught the ball. The catch caused a long argument, but it was allowed and then the umpire stopped the game until the ladder was removed.

(Copyright, 1911, by Joseph E. Bowles.)

This sounds like a true story to me. Ping Bodie hit 30 home runs for the San Francisco Seals in 1910. A typical league-leading figure in that era was more like 12 to 15.

WANT MORE BILL JAMES?

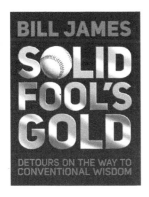

SOLID FOOL'S GOLD
Detours on the Way to Conventional Wisdom
by Bill James

Plenty of articles on baseball-including hot pitchers, "late career" players, the predictability of RBI, the 33 best starting rotations and the worst teams of all time—along with other witty, insightful, and just plain fun musings by Bill James.

THE BILL JAMES HANDBOOK
by Bill James and the staff of Baseball Info Solutions

For 25 years, *The Bill James Handbook* has been the first, best, and most complete annual baseball reference guide available. New sections include: No-Hitter Summary; Home-Run Robberies; Scouting Report; and Hitter Analysis. Updated sections include: Career Baserunning and Pitch Repertoire.

HOW BILL JAMES CHANGED
OUR VIEW OF BASEBALL
By Colleagues, Critics, Competitors,
and Just Plain Fans
Edited by Gregory F. Augustine Pierce

Twelve original articles by John Dewan, Gary Huckabay, Susan McCarthy, Steve Moyer, Daryl Morey, Rob Neyer, Hal Richman, Alan Schwarz, Ron Shandler, Dave Studenmund, John Thorn, and Sam Walker, with a "Last Word" by Bill James and testimony by lots of fans whose lives were changed by reading his work.